A Marine Remembers

A Marine Remembers

Samuel Rimler

N. Charles Sylvan Company, Publishers
Martinez, California

Rimler, Samuel, 1912-1999
A Marine Remembers
ISBN 1-886-385-00-9

Library of Congress Control Number:
2002115873

Copyright © 2003 by
N. Charles Sylvan Company

All rights reserved. No part of this publication may be reproduced, stored in a retrieval system or transmitted in any form or by any means, electronic, mechanical, photocopying, recording or otherwise, without prior written permission of the publisher.

Cover photo: Samuel Rimler in Guantanamo Bay, Cuba circa 1931, photographer unknown but said to have been Margaret Bourke-White

Jacket design by Chris Jones

First printing, October 2003

Contents

Introduction	*vii*
The Recruit	1
The Jewish Question	6
The Dentist and the Patient	9
The Constipated DI	11
The Scribe	13
The Transformation	15
The Rifle	17
The Southerner and the Gangster	19
The Gambler	23
The Metamorphosis	26
The Escape	28
The Beginning	30
The Good Samaritan	33
The Perplexed Marine	35
The Major General	40
The Private and the General	42
The Amateur Boxer and the Street Fighter	45
The Family	47
The Blessing in Disguise	51
The Earthquake	54
The Power of the Bayonet	56
The Tidal Wave	58
The Ensign	60
A Penny Saved is a Penny Lost	64
The Coal Miner and the East-Sider	66
The Ham Sandwich	67
The Bridge of Sighs	75

The Reunion	77
The Pitiless Sea	80
The Arrangement	82
The Teacher	84
The Sin of Omission	88
The Reluctant Chief	91
The Retreads and the WAVES	93
The Blackboard	95
The Message	97
The Circumcision	100
The Fire At Sea	103
The Moral Binding	105
The Chiefs	108
Brother, Can You Spare a Cigarette?	111
The Kiss	112
The Passenger	114
The Captain and the Chiefs	117
The Enigma	119
The Decision	121
The Last Hurrah	122
The In-Laws	124
The Friends	126
The Fall From Grace	130
The Guilt Complex—Part I	132
The Guilt Complex—Part II	133

Introduction

These stories were written in the early 1990s when the author was in his early 80s. He wrote them so his grandchildren and their children would know what he had done as a young man. As it turns out, it is a document for everyone else as well.

It presents a picture, perhaps unique, of what it was like to be a Jewish immigrant in the U.S. Marine Corps during the years between the world wars, when the Corps had just seventeen-thousand men, mostly Southerners, and was led by the charismatic Major General Smedley Butler.

The author never knew his age exactly. Ellis Island Registry records say he was ten when he arrived in New York Harbor from Logov, Poland in 1920. More likely, he was eight. He was the sixth and youngest child of Jacov Josef Rimler and Ruchel Nussbaum. Jacov Josef came to America first, at some point between 1912 and 1914, bringing with him his two elder sons, Eddie and Israel, and leaving his wife behind with their four younger: Sylvia, Abraham, Mildred, and Samuel. While Jacov Josef and the two older boys were in the U.S. earning money to book passage for the rest of the family, World War I intervened. Those were years when Ruchel had to shepherd her children as they were confronted by, and trapped between, opposing armies, Russian and German, who despised

Jews even more than they hated one another.

The author rarely discussed those days and he does not write about them here. All we know for certain is that Ruchel broke down under the stress and made an unsuccessful attempt on her life by throwing herself into a well. She never regained her mental balance and eventually died in a New York asylum. We also know that Samuel, aged five, went from door to door singing songs in exchange for food.

When the family was reunited in New York City in the early 1920s, it had no center. Everyone made his or her own way. The author left school after the eighth grade and found himself on the streets, sleeping in pool halls, and leaning toward petty thievery as an acceptable occupation. That is where we find him as these tales (he called them vignettes) begin.

He takes us through four years as a private in the regular Marine Corps (1930 to 1934), two as a sergeant in the Marine Reserves (1939 to 1941), and four as a chief petty officer in the Navy during World War II. He ends his story with the end of World War II. He was to live another fifty-four years, but was most proud of his years in the service—proud and, paradoxically, ashamed. He never forgave himself for not being with his old Marine battalion when it landed on Guadalcanal. The fact that he was aboard ship in the North Atlantic at the time doing convoy duty did not assuage his guilt.

As will become clear from these memoirs, he held himself to a very high—perhaps an impossibly high—standard. After all, he was a Marine.

He was also a loving husband to his wife, Ruth, and father to us, his children.

Rona Arato
Walter Rimler

The Recruit

It was a hot July morning in 1930 and I was walking east on 23rd Street. I had just been fired from my job at a stationery store for dishonesty.

Earlier, while sweeping the store, I had spotted a crumpled two-dollar bill under a counter and had pocketed it. The money had been deliberately placed there by the owner to test my honesty and I had failed the test. Now I walked the streets without a job, without purpose, and without direction.

As I neared Lexington Avenue, my eyes were attracted to a poster of a Marine in dress blues. Reflections of the movie *What Price Glory?* flashed through my mind and I came closer to get a better look.

A sergeant exited the doorway and stationed himself beside the poster. He seemed unaware of the unkempt young man as he stood there nonchalantly gazing at the street scene.

For a few moments we stood there: a school dropout overawed by the sight of the real and pictured Marines in their dress blue uniforms with all manner of colored ribbons on their chests, and the sergeant who seemed not to be aware of my presence. Then our eyes made contact.

"Want to join the Marines?" the sergeant asked.

I, not believing that the remark was addressed to me, looked about to see if there was anyone else present. But nobody else was there.

"What do you say?" the sergeant inquired in a Southern drawl.

"Do you think I can?" I asked doubtfully.

"Why don't we go upstairs and see," the sergeant suggested.

"I'd like to try," I said.

We walked up the rickety steps of the one-story brick building and the sergeant opened the first door at the head of the stairs. Inside, an officer sitting behind a desk leafing through a magazine glanced up but paid us no further attention. A small desk on the side of the room and a table in the rear with two straight-backed chairs behind it were the only other pieces of furniture in the office. The sergeant handed me a form to fill out, pointed to the table in back of the room, and then seated himself behind the unoccupied desk and pretended to look busy.

I sat at the table and studied the form, making no attempt to write. There were questions on it that I couldn't, or was ashamed to answer. The officer, noticing my inactivity, glanced toward the sergeant, who approached me. "Having trouble?" he inquired. I shook my head in the negative and bent over the form.

There was the question of date of birth. I didn't know when I was born. Nobody had ever told me. So I opted for April 15th, the middle of the month in which Passover usually falls, having once overheard that I had been born before, during, or after Passover.

A Marine Remembers

Then there was age. That was another dilemma. Not knowing when I was born, I didn't know my age. Remembering that the year before, a friend and I had been kicked out of an Army recruiting office because of our youth, I put down twenty, not wanting that to happen again.

There was the question of education. Having dropped out of the eighth grade of junior high school, I was ashamed to admit it. So I just put down high school, omitting the junior.

And then there was the question of occupation. I had no occupation. Remembering a poem I had learned in school entitled "Work" by Henry Van Dyke, in which the poet praised all manner of labor, I put down laborer, figuring that what was good for Henry Van Dyke was good enough for me.

The only other question that bothered me was place of birth. Having been born in Poland, I was ashamed to admit it. But I put it down anyway. The rest of the information I had to provide was elementary and I had no problem filling in the spaces.

When I was finished filling out the form, I glanced up at the sergeant who came over, took it from me, looked at it, and then took it to the officer for his inspection. The officer studied it for a minute and then said, "He'll have to get his parents' permission."

My heart sank when I heard the officer's remarks. Parents' permission? How could I hope to do that?

Samuel Rimler

My father, an orthodox and observant man with a full grown beard who spent all of his spare time in shul, would just as soon have given me permission to apostatize as to join. For men of his belief, Jews don't voluntarily join the military—they run away from doing so—even if they have to run to America.

My mother, who had suffered a breakdown in Poland and whose condition had worsened since coming to the United States, now sat either staring silently out the window or sitting on the stoop of our tenement house, singing.

The sergeant approached me. "Did you hear what the lieutenant said?" he asked.

"Both parents?" I asked hopelessly.

The sergeant glanced questioningly at the lieutenant who held up one finger.

Just one, I thought. There was hope. My mother used to sign my report cards in Yiddish, not knowing what she was signing. If I found her in a more lucid moment I was sure I could get her to sign the application form. But she could only write Yiddish. "Would a signature in Yiddish be valid?" I asked the sergeant.

"A signature in what?" the sergeant asked incredulously.

"It would be valid if it was witnessed," the officer called out.

The sergeant and I boarded a street car and got off at 5th Street and Avenue A, the other passengers believing that I was being taken into custody. As we walked east on 5th Street to-

A Marine Remembers

wards the East River, the men on the sidewalk hastened to make room for us and the women clucked their tongues, while all this time I was praying that my father wouldn't be home and that I wouldn't find my mother sitting on the stoop of the house, singing. When we crossed Avenue D I glanced toward our house. My mother was not sitting on the steps. I breathed a sigh of relief. But there was still the problem of my father. Would I find him home?

We walked up the three flights of stairs of the tenement house and I cautiously opened the door of the apartment and peered inside. My father wasn't home and my mother sat silently by the window.

I walked over to her, the sergeant a step behind me. I handed her the application form and the sergeant's fountain pen. "Mama," I said in Yiddish, "sign this," pointing to the place for her signature.

"Like I did the others?" she asked.

"Like you did the others, Mama," I said.

She signed her name in Yiddish in the designated place, the sergeant affixed his signature bearing witness, I kissed my mother on the cheek, and we left the house.

Within forty-eight hours, I arrived at the Marine base, Parris Island, South Carolina, a place I had never heard of and would never forget.

Samuel Rimler

The Jewish Question

  On July 25, 1930, the day I was sworn into the Marine Corps, the Corps' strength was seventeen thousand officers and men. Of that number, it was doubtful if among them could be found twenty-five Marines of Jewish heritage. If there were that many in the Corps, they would have been scattered throughout the world. The odds against finding a Jewish Marine on Parris Island other than myself were pretty great. And yet, there was one. And he would, in time, put me in a very awkward position.

  After my platoon was sworn in, we congregated near the supply depot at the Main Station, waiting to be issued uniforms and equipment before being turned over to the drill instructors who would have charge over us for the ensuing seven weeks. (We were given three choices regarding the disposal of our civilian clothes. We could mail them home, sell them to the post civilian tailor, or discard them. I discarded mine as they were worthless.)

  As I sat outside the supply depot chatting with one of the other recruits, a tall, rangy fellow approached. "He's from Tennessee," the recruit I was chatting with informed me.

  When the tall recruit from the Volunteer State got close he looked at me and said, "Hello, Jew."

  I was about to stand up and challenge him when my companion whispered, "He didn't mean anything by it. He is trying to be friendly.

A Marine Remembers

It's like saying hello, Dutch or hello, Swede."

I responded, "Hello, Davy Crockett."

We both laughed, shook hands, and that was the end of it.

It wasn't until after I had left boot camp that the question of my religion was made an issue. And the situation that brought it about was not of my making.

Mine was the last platoon to go through boot camp that year and by the time we got through, all outgoing details had been assigned. This meant that I was stuck on the island and given alternating weeks of mess duty and guard duty, the most undesirable kinds of duty imaginable.

On a Sunday afternoon, on one of my rare days off, I was lying on my bunk reading, completely undressed except for my skivvies. There were a number of other Marines in the squad room lazing about, some reading, some writing letters, and others putting in some sack time.

My bunk was away from the door, so I didn't see a Marine dressed in full uniform, a stranger to me, saunter into the room. But I soon heard him.

"Anyone for Milky Ways?" he asked, digging his hand into the brown paper bag he was carrying.

A couple of Marines obligingly took a Milky Way from him, but one took umbrage. "What're you trying to do, buy friends?" he asked.

"Not at all," the other protested. "I'm just

trying to be friendly, take one," he insisted, handing him the piece of candy.

It was knocked out of his hand. "I told you I didn't want it," was the response, "and quit your pandering."

"You didn't have to do that," the donor protested.

"Do you want to step outside and do something about it?" was the challenge.

"I don't want to fight you," was the reply.

"I didn't think so. You're yellow. You're a yellow Jew." Then, becoming braver by the other's lack of response, he added, "All Jews are yellow."

When he used the word Jews all eyes in the squad room turned to me. Up until this point, I had studiously kept my eyes glued to the book I had been reading, trying to make believe I wasn't hearing what was being said. I didn't like the intruder with his bag of candy, didn't like his looks, didn't like his behavior, and didn't like the fact that he was permitting himself to take all those insults.

The last thing I wanted to do was to get into a fight. But now, with all eyes gazing in my direction, I knew I had to act. Otherwise, the rest of the men in the squad room would look down on me.

Reluctantly, I put on my socks, then my shoes, then my trousers. I walked over to the snide Marine and said, "Come outside, I'll fight you."

"I have no quarrel with you," the other

A Marine Remembers

said.

"I thought I heard you say all Jews were yellow. I thought you were looking for a fight."

"Well, I didn't mean it that way."

"Next time say what you mean," I said. Then, turning to the Marine with the candy, I said, "Why don't you go back to your own barracks?"

In my ensuing years in both Marine Corps and Navy, the question of my religion was never raised again.

The Dentist and the Patient

I had never owned a toothbrush. As far as I knew, nobody in my house had ever owned a toothbrush. The first toothbrush I owned was the one issued to me when I enlisted in the Marine Corps.

After being sworn in, each recruit was issued a ditty bag containing toilet supplies including a toothbrush and straight razor. The cost, five dollars, was to be deducted from the first month's pay. The straight razor was probably surplus property left over from the First World War that the government wanted to rid itself of at the expense of the recruits.

In view of the fact that I had never owned a toothbrush and had never even attempted to brush my teeth, it was little less than remarkable that the only bad tooth in my mouth was a back molar that needed to be extracted. This extraction would try the mettle of the owner and the extractor.

It was the morning of my second week at boot camp when I was summoned to the dentist's office located adjacent to the sick bay at the recruit depot. The dentist, a lieutenant in the Navy, directed me to be seated in the dentist's chair, a contraption I had never seen before. He whistled while he worked, getting his instruments together. As he approached me we eyed each other warily, neither of us knowing what to expect from the other.

Perhaps Novocain had not yet been invented, perhaps it was in short supply, perhaps it was thought that Marines didn't require it. In any event, none was given this recruit. The dentist began to tap the tainted tooth with a pair of pliers, softly whistling under his breath. It was hard to know if the whistling was meant to bolster his courage or mine.

And then the battle was joined, the dentist trying to extract the molar, the molar resisting its displacement, and the recruit, in pain, trapped between the two antagonists.

After several minutes of pulling, the dentist stopped trying. He also stopped whistling. I, suffering in silence, feared that I was causing the dentist too much distress.

After a few moments' respite, the dentist tried again. This time, after much pulling, the tooth broke and he was able to extract part of the molar.

Again there was a short respite, the dentist looking quizzically at me and I, still much in pain, hoping that what was happening would not be a mark against my record.

The third time proved to be more successful. We braced ourselves and after an indeterminate length of time and much effort, the dentist extracted the molar and held it up to my view.

"I wish all my patients were like you," he said, handing me a piece of paper which would relieve me of all duties for the rest of the day. "Some patients would rather face a firing squad than a dentist."

The Constipated DI

In the Marine Corps hierarchy, there is no one lower than a boot. Once he is sworn in and relegated to boot camp, the drill instructors take over and he becomes the most helpless and hapless individual in the Corps. The boot has no free time or free will. The drill instructors dominate his life and he is under constant observation. Every minute of his time is accounted for and he can do nothing without their direction.

The Marine Corps does not permit or condone mistreatment inflicted on the drill instructor's vulnerable charges, but it does stress discipline. The boot can only speak when spoken to. Drill instructors, whether they are acting corporals or acting sergeants, have to be addressed as "Sir." And the boot may only refer to himself in the third person, such as:

"Sir, in answer to the sergeant's question, Private Jones does not know how many lands and grooves are in his rifle."

Nor do the drill instructors have an easy time of it. To take sixty men from all walks of life and every section of the country, who have never had any military training or experience, and in less than two months mold them into an efficient fighting unit, is an exasperating task. And sometimes a DI is not up to the task and takes his exasperation out on his vulnerable charges.

In the summer of 1930 when I went through boot camp, mine was the last platoon to go through the process for the year. The Marine Corps had reached its full strength of 17,000 officers and men.

Three drill instructors saw us through: two acting sergeants whose forebears must have fought in the War Between the States and an acting corporal, a six-foot three-inch two hundred twenty-pound hulk of a man who didn't observe the rules of conduct. While the platoon was marching on the drill field, their uniforms soaked with perspiration, he would invariably march alongside the men and elbow them in the ribs. These acts were made for no apparent reason and were repeated time and again. And there was no recourse. The other DIs, if they were aware of his actions, pretended not to be. And then nature came to our aid.

A Marine Remembers

Our platoon was standing at attention on the drill field, the merciless South Carolina sun beating down on us, waiting to be inspected by the Marine gunner, a warrant officer who had charge over the entire boot camp operation. The two hundred twenty-pound hulk stood three paces forward in front of me. He had held that position for the better part of an hour. Suddenly, he started to sway.

For a moment I thought that I was swaying and that the drill instructor was standing at attention. And then, just as suddenly, the figure in front of me dropped like a sack of potatoes. No one moved to come to his aid. Neither did the Marine gunner pay him any heed.

When inspection was over, he was helped off the field. "I haven't moved my bowels in two days," he was overheard to say by way of apology.

Following that incident, there were no more elbowings.

The Scribe

There were sixty-two men in my platoon when our group photograph was taken in boot camp on August 8, 1930. Every recruit was issued a copy of the photograph, the price to be deducted from our monthly pay of $20.80. (The pay was actually $21.00, but twenty cents were turned over to the Navy for hospitalization.]

One of the recruits had mailed the photograph to his girl friend in Evansville, Indiana, who in turn showed it to her Jewish girlfriend.

How the Jewish girlfriend was able to pick me out as the only Jewish recruit was beyond my understanding. But she did and asked her girlfriend to ask her boyfriend to ask me to correspond with her. This I agreed to do. She mailed me her name, address, a picture of herself and permission, when writing, to address her by her given name of Lilyan.

At the same time, I received another request. It was from a recruit of Polish origin, another member of my platoon. In somewhat the same circumstances, he had received a letter from a girl named Wanda of Passaic, New Jersey, asking him to correspond with her. But he had a problem. He wasn't, as he expressed it, "edjicated" enough to write to this intelligent and good-looking girl. Would I write to her for him, he asked. I would, I replied, for the price of a Milky Way per letter. So the deal was struck.

All during boot camp, and for months thereafter, Wanda's letters were shown to me and I replied to them in my own handwriting.

I had always been good in composition. I got that way by reading. And so both women, Lilyan of Evansville and Wanda of Passaic, enjoyed reading my letters. And I enjoyed writing to them, although if truth be told, I favored Wanda over Lilyan. She, judging by their photos, looked younger and prettier. Judging by her letters, she seemed more intelligent than the girl in Evansville. Given a choice, I would have gladly swapped girls with the Marine for whom I was writing, even if it meant the loss of my source of Milky Ways.

But my correspondence with Wanda came to an abrupt halt when I slipped and fell on my head at the Main Station mess hall and spent the better part of a month at the Navy hospital.

After my discharge from the hospital, I contacted the Marine for whom I had done the letter writing and inquired as to the well-being of Wanda.

"I don't know," he said.

"Why don't you know?" I asked.

"After you stopped writing to her," he said, "she gave me the gate. She insisted that I give her the name of the Marine with whom she was corresponding and I refused to do so."

In a way, we had both lost her. I had enjoyed corresponding with Wanda of Passaic, New Jersey.

The Transformation

    Military Discipline, Courtesies,
       and Customs of Service

The military salute is a respectful greeting exchanged between two self-respecting members of the same profession. It is the chief mark by which the well-trained and well-disciplined military man can be distinguished. A man who renders the required salute promptly and proudly displays the right spirit. He can be counted upon to perform all his duties in the same spirit. Exceptions to this are rare.

The rendering of the salute is not an acknowledgment of inferiority, anymore than it is to speak first to an acquaintance. Regulations require that the salute be rendered by both the junior and senior. It is only natural that the junior should salute first. When saluting an officer, hold yourself erect, look him in the eye and say, "Good morning, sir," or "Good evening, sir," as the case may be.

I remembered those military instructions as I walked quick-time to my radio class at Marine Barracks, Quantico, Virginia, when approaching me, some thirty paces away, was Major General Smedley D. Butler, the base commander, holder of two Congressional Medals of Honor, and by far the most famous and decorated Marine in the Corps' proud history.

Barely a year before, I had been slouching along the streets of New York, slovenly-dressed, unkempt, unemployed, and uncertain of the future. Now, cleanliness and neatness of dress marked my appearance. My head held high, I was about to cross paths with the most famous general of the time.

As regulations required, when I came to within six paces of the general, I saluted promptly and smartly and said, "Good morning, sir."

The general, just as promptly and

A Marine Remembers

smartly, returned my salute and said, "Good morning," after which both Marines continued on to their respective destinations.

The Rifle

I had never handled a firearm. Before joining the Marine Corps, I had never even owned a toy pistol. I much admired the cowboys in the movies such as Tom Mix, Art Accord, Hoot Gibson and the like who, no matter what the distance, or how fast they were traveling on their mounts, or what direction they were facing, could hit a target (usually an Indian) without effort. (In reality, they had as much chance of hitting the Indian under those circumstances as the Indian had of getting his land back.)

The first rifle I handled was the one issued to me after I joined the Marine Corps. It was a 30-caliber 1903 Springfield rifle used in France during the American Expeditionary Force's participation in World War I.

After my platoon's first four weeks at boot camp, we were transferred to the rifle range and placed under the jurisdiction of the rifle range coaches for three weeks. It was up to the coaches, each an expert rifleman, to take our platoon of raw recruits and teach us what the rifle was really meant for.

The men were taught about windage, elevation, adjustment of the rear sight (the front sight was not adjustable), squeezing the trigger, how to line up the sights so the rifle was aimed at the base of the target, and most important, how to adjust the rifle sling so the rifle would become a part of the Marine who fired it.

During the first two weeks on the range, not a single round of live ammunition was issued. The time was taken up with instructions and dry runs. But the third week would be for record.

Seventy rounds of ammunition would be issued to each recruit, to be fired from 200 to 600 yard ranges. At six hundred yards, the ten-inch bull's eye looked like the period at the end of a sentence.

When it was my turn to go to the firing line, the order was given, "Ready on the left, ready on the right, unlock, ready on the firing line," after which the targets upped and the firing began.

I did everything right, but I was just missing the bull's eye, hitting instead the circles around it. I suspected that there was something wrong with my rear sight and complained to the rifle coach who shrugged me off. The result was that I failed to qualify as a marksman, only one of five members of my platoon who failed to do so.

The next time I fired for record was at Fort Lewis, Washington, where my friend Kusheba, who had preceded me and made sharpshooter, allowed me to use his rifle. I made expert rifleman without any trouble, which netted me five dollars a month extra pay for the following twelve months.

For the next several months, I tried every which way to have my rifle surveyed (exchanged or taken out of service), but it was an impossible task. Then I gave up trying. It would have been easier, I thought, for a Catholic to get a divorce.

The Southerner and the Gangster

Mine was the last platoon to go through boot camp in the summer of 1930 and I was stuck on the island, all details having been dispatched to bases around the globe where Marine contingents were stationed. This meant that I was relegated to alternate weeks of mess duty and guard duty without letup.

I was doing mess duty at the main station mess hall which serviced some three hundred Marines stationed on the island. These were other unfortunates, like me, who were stuck there awaiting transfer. It was during that period that something happened to me that had never happened before and has never happened since. I was knocked unconscious (an experience that tended to make me doubt the existence of a hereafter).

Mess duty was hard and tedious work. Starting before reveille and sometimes lasting until after taps (depending on the good will of the chief mess man, a corporal in charge of the mess hall), the mess men, each assigned to a station, had to scrub their wooden tables, set them, serve and wait on the men seated at them, make sure the serving dishes were full at all times, clean up, and then repeat the process for the next meal. That being done, they then had to clean the mess hall, scrub and wash the tile deck, and clean flies off the window screens. (One bright young Marine had the idea of wiring the screens to electrocute the flies.) Following that, and after a rigid inspection by the chief mess man, if approved, the mess men were permitted to repair to their barracks between meals and sack out for as long as time permitted them to do so, after which they had to return to the mess hall.

The mess men were responsible for all dishes, cups, saucers, and silverware at their stations. If a dish, cup, saucer, or other such item was broken, the chief mess man would make a note of it and the cost of same would be deducted from their monthly pay. The same held true for silverware. All knives, forks, tablespoons, and teaspoons had to be accounted for, or else paid for by the luckless mess men. Consequently, before leaving the mess hall, each mess man's station had to be inspected by the chief mess man to make sure that all dishes and silverware were accounted for. What happened to those items after the mess man left the premises and his station had been inspected was not his responsibility.

One day, after noonday chow, I was carrying a tray of dirty dishes to the rear of the mess hall when both my feet gave way. I fell backwards onto the soapy tile deck that was being swabbed, the back of my head hitting the deck, and the dirty dishes piling on top of me. My first thought as I was being helped to my feet was: are there any broken dishes? How much is this going to cost me?

Before I had a chance to take inventory, the chief mess man was at my side. "Are you hurt?" he asked. I shook my head, still concerned about the breakage. "Do you want to go to the sick bay?" the chief mess man asked. Again I shook my head. "You're going anyway," the chief mess man said, and summoning another mess man, ordered, "Accompany this man to the sick bay." And that's all I remembered.

When I next opened my eyes, I found myself in bed in a small private room with my head splitting as if it would come apart. A blond, blue-eyed Marine was staring intently at me. "Where am I?" I asked.

"You're at the United States Naval Hospital," the blond Marine said. "You were brought here unconscious yesterday afternoon and you've suffered a concussion."

I closed my eyes, hoping that my headache would go away, hoping that the blue-eyed Marine would go away. But when I opened them again, they were both still with me. "What the hell are you staring at?" I demanded to know when the other wouldn't remove his eyes from me.

"I want to see what a New York gangster looks like," was the droll reply. 'Now, how about something to eat?"

I wanted to reply in kind to the other's remark, but my head was throbbing and I had gotten used to the Southern brand of drollery. "I'd rather vomit," I said.

"Just a little chicken broth?" the other suggested.

"Where would you get chicken broth?" I wanted to know.

"I have charge of the diet kitchen adjacent to your room; I'll go and get you some chicken broth and maybe a cracker or two," and with those words, he left me to myself. When he returned, he was carrying a tray with a bowl of chicken broth and a handful of crackers, and after propping me up, spoon-fed me the broth and forced me to eat a couple of soda crackers. After that he left the room.

And that's how I met Richard Hampton Thornton of Charlotte, North Carolina, one of the two closest friends I made while in the Marine Corps. It was Thornton who later urged me to write to his sister in Charlotte.

Private Thornton had enlisted in the Marine Corps a year before me, had gone to cooks and bakers school, become a cook at the main station mess hall, had gone on liberty to Beaufort, S.C., had met the nicest, most innocent-looking girl he had ever seen, and though it wasn't for free, had had sex with her, returning with a dose of gonorrhea. While in the hospital

A Marine Remembers

he had charge of the diet kitchen in "D" Ward, the venereal ward where I had been placed, there being no other beds available. I was the only patient there without a venereal disease.

When my Southern friend was discharged from the hospital, I succeeded him in the diet kitchen. And when I was discharged, we were inseparable until I left Parris Island to go to radio school at Quantico, Virginia.

The Gambler

The Marine Corps is older than the country it serves. It was organized on November 10, 1775, a year before the Declaration of Independence, twelve years before the Constitutional Convention. It was traditional on that date for the Corps to serve special chow and cigarettes to celebrate its founding.

On November 10, 1930, to celebrate that founding, the patients, of whom I was one, at the United States Naval Hospital on Parris Island, were issued packages of cigarettes along with the holiday meal.

In those days, everybody smoked. Even in the movies, everybody smoked. Often, when a soldier on the battlefield was depicted dying of his wounds, a buddy stuck a lighted cigarette into his mouth. It was the expected thing to do. Whether it did the dying soldier good or harm was not the issue. It was the expected thing to do.

But in Ward "D" at the Naval hospital to which I was consigned because no beds in any of the other wards were available, where all of the patients were afflicted with syphilis or gonorrhea, I being the exception, only my friend Thornton and I didn't smoke. So a poker game was organized, the cigarettes to be used in lieu of money.

Since my friend knew nothing about the game, we pooled our resources and I was the player, my friend watching over my shoulders. The poker game lasted the greater part of the day, with a break for evening chow, and when it ended shortly before taps, I had won every cigarette in the ward. We were in possession of a mound of loose cigarettes, too many to count, and we did not know what to do with them. After a short confab we decided to return all of the cigarettes to their original owners. We included our own in the distribution.

Three weeks after that event, after I had assumed charge of the diet kitchen when my friend was discharged from the hospital to assume his duties as a cook at the Main Station mess hall, the Marine paymaster arrived at the hospital to distribute our pay, each according to his rating. My pay amounted to $20.80, less $2.50 that had been deducted for dishes broken while I was a mess man at the same mess hall where my friend was now assigned as a cook.

With all that money floating around and nowhere to spend it, another poker game was

A Marine Remembers

organized, this time with real money. And this time, the game, as far as I was concerned, was not all that time-consuming.

I had always considered myself a good poker player. It was a game I had played night and day on the sidewalks of the East Side of New York. I could keep track of the fifty-two cards in the deck, which gave me an edge.

The game was open poker and, as luck would have it, the first two cards dealt me were kings back to back, one showing and the other hidden. The other players dropped out, but the Naval hospital corpsman saw me all the way. When the fifth card was dealt, my hand was not improved, but the corpsman was dealt an ace.

"What's your bet?" the corpsman asked.

"It's your bet," I replied, "you're high."

The corpsman looked at my table stakes and counted fourteen dollars and seventy five cents. "That's my bet," he said.

I thought a while and tried to size up the situation, while the onlookers stood aside and watched.

That last card, the ace that the corpsman had been dealt, had changed the entire situation. Supposing he had an ace in the hole? But what were the odds of him having an ace in the hole?

One ace showed on the table, the last card dealt the corpsman. But there were three other aces not accounted for. What were the odds of him having one of them hidden?

I looked at the deck in the dealer's hand

and judged there to be about thirty cards. The chances of the three missing aces being in the remainder of the pack were one in ten. Those were not good odds, especially when I considered that if I lost the pot I wouldn't see another dime until next pay day, a month away. I was about to fold and concede the pot to the hospital corpsman.

But then I thought about it. There was a lot of money in the pot and the corpsman might be bluffing. And there were all those people watching.

That last thought decided me. I was not about to be bluffed by a Navy corpsman. Before giving myself a chance to think otherwise, I pushed my $14.75 into the pot and said, "I see you."

As soon as I did, the corpsman turned over his other card and it was the ace of spades.

I did not see another dime until the following pay day.

The Metamorphosis

The rank of Marine gunner is neither fish nor fowl. He's neither an officer nor an enlisted man. Although he may well be the most knowledgeable man in a unit, by virtue of time served and experience, he must still salute and, on occasion, take orders from the greenest shave tail (2nd lieutenant). His insignia is a bursting bomb, he's entitled to wear half a Sam Browne

A Marine Remembers

belt, is equipped with a saber, and rates a salute from enlisted men whatever their rating.

When I went through boot camp during the months of July, August, and September of 1930, Marine Gunner Jenks was in overall charge of the camp and the drill instructors were as alert to his demands as the boots over whom they had charge were alert to theirs, for their careers rested on the Marine gunner's judgment and recommendations.

When reviewing troops in the field, Marine Gunner Jenks drew his saber to return the salutes of the DIs as the men passed in review (men in ranks didn't salute; they executed the command eyes right). Although of average height, a little on in years, and somewhat fleshy—with stomach drawn in, shoulders back and height stretched to the fullest, the Marine gunner, although just a warrant officer, could well have been a major general by the way he comported himself.

I had no occasion to see the Marine gunner again until several weeks after leaving boot camp. The change in him was astonishing.

I had been put in charge of the diet kitchen at the Naval hospital in Ward D, the venereal ward, being the only patient in that ward not so afflicted. The diet kitchen was located in the forward part of the ward. It was kept locked and the key was always in my possession.

I awoke one morning to find I had a new patient. The newcomer had been brought in during the early hours of the morning and was housed in "the cage"—a six by six foot cell located in the rear section of the ward and used to accommodate a sick prisoner. To my utter amazement, the occupant was none other than Marine Gunner Jenks. He had been arrested for drunkenness and wife beating and had been placed in the hospital cell for observation.

Clad in hospital garb, unshaven, red-eyed, stomach protruding without benefit of corset, he lacked boots, uniform, saber and military bearing. He looked like a tired, beaten, little old man. He was like an oyster out of its shell.

"Can I have bacon and eggs for breakfast?" he inquired meekly when I introduced myself.

"Yes, sir," was the response.

At that, the Marine gunner's back seemed to straighten somewhat.

The Escape

Guard duty, mess duty; mess duty, guard duty; there seemed no letup for me from those rigorous and mundane jobs. I was confined to the hospital for over four weeks, ostensibly for observation relating to my concussion, but actually because the doctor wanted me there.

Upon my discharge from the hospital, my friend Richard Hampton Thornton recommended that I be assigned to take his place in the diet kitchen and his recommendation was

A Marine Remembers

approved by the doctor in charge of the ward.

The first Saturday after I had taken charge, just before captain's inspection, I happened on a jar of metal polish and polished the silverware until it gleamed. When the captain inspected the kitchen, his eyes were drawn to the sparkling silverware. He was so impressed by what he saw that he complimented the doctor, promising him a letter of commendation. I, on the other hand, standing at attention alongside the table where the plates and silverware were displayed, fervently prayed that the captain wouldn't handle the silverware and have the polish come off on his white gloves. When that didn't happen I breathed a sigh of relief and after the two officers left, I quickly washed the silverware with soap and water.

But after the incident of the shining silverware, there was no way the doctor would approve of my discharge from the hospital. He kept me there until he couldn't think of any more excuses to prevent me from leaving. So it was guard duty, mess duty, guard duty, mess duty all over again.

Every day I looked at the bulletin board in my barracks to see if there were impending outgoing details and every day I was doomed to disappointment. It seemed that the Marine Corps had forgotten about me. With Marines stationed all over the globe and on every capital ship in the fleet, they couldn't find a place for me. I felt like a pariah. I was stuck on the island without being permanently stationed there.

Samuel Rimler

Although my work was strenuous, I was gaining weight. My friend Thornton, who was a cook at the Main Station mess hall, had access to the mess hall larder. He would sneak out all kinds of canned fruits and all flavors of ice cream and we two would find secluded spots and gorge ourselves. That, too, troubled me. Not having a taste for beer, I didn't want to acquire a beer belly.

One morning, I looked at the bulletin board and saw that applications were being accepted for telephone school. I would have applied for any school to get off the island and away from the regimen of mess duty, guard duty. But when I applied, I was too late. Too many other unfortunates had beaten me to the job.

As a consolation, however, I was assigned to radio school. After a short stint at a radio class on the island, where I was taught the Morse Code and touch typing, I was transferred to the Signal Battalion at Quantico, Virginia to further my studies.

Before leaving the island, my friend, the Southerner, and I had a last repast of ice cream, cake and canned fruits, shook hands, bade each other goodbye, and never saw each other again.

The Beginning

In the spring of 1931 at Quantico, Virginia, the First Separate Training Battalion was formed. It was to be the forerunner of the Fleet

A Marine Remembers

Marine Force, or FMF, as it was generally referred to.

This battalion was to board the battleships *Wyoming* and *Arkansas*. The *Wyoming* would head for Galveston, the *Arkansas* for New Orleans, and the Marines would participate in each city's annual Mardi Gras parade. We would then rendezvous at Guantanamo Bay, Cuba to await further orders.

Scuttlebutt had it that the Marines would then head for the Panama Canal, thence to the Far East to forestall the Japanese takeover of Manchuria.

Our first night at sea was off Cape Hatteras, one of the roughest pieces of water on the planet, and almost without exception, the Marines became seasick. Stationed aboard the *Wyoming*, I developed a migraine headache, crawled into a corner of one of the ship's bulkheads and tried to sleep it off. But sleep on the overcrowded ship was impossible. So I sat up all night nursing my headache. When morning came, my headache had subsided, but I got as close as I ever came to being seasick during my five years at sea with the Marine Corps and the Navy.

By the time the two battleships reached Guantanamo Bay, orders had been changed. The new orders directed that the Marines stationed on the *Wyoming* be transferred to the *Arkansas*, the *Arkansas* to leave for the West Coast to join the Pacific Fleet, and the *Wyoming* to remain on the East Coast.

On the *Arkansas*, no provision had been made for our arrival. Our living conditions were unbearable. We lived out of our sea bags, slept head to toe on the bare decks, and used our clothes for pillows. Each Marine was allotted one bucket of fresh, cold water each morning with which to brush his teeth, shave and shower.

And the lines were perennial. There were lines for morning, noon and evening chow. Lines to go to the head. Lines to collect toilet paper before getting to the head. Lines to the various scuttlebutts aboard ship to get a drink of fresh water.

And then there were the dashes. A dash to be first in line for chow or the head or for the single bucket of fresh water each morning. And last but foremost, a dash to find a place on deck to spread out and go to sleep without having another Marine's feet stuck in your face.

Conditions didn't improve until weeks after the battleship's arrival on the West Coast, when folding cots were provided, lockers assigned, and places made available to store our sea bags. Then, if the living wasn't easy, it was at least easier.

The USS *Arkansas* was to be my home for the next two and a half years, longer than any home I had occupied on land without interruption since coming to America.

A Marine Remembers

The Good Samaritan

Sometimes to gain the respect of your peers you act on impulse and do something foolish. Such was the situation in my case in early 1931.

The First Separate Training Battalion, the forerunner of the Fleet Marine Force, was formed at Quantico and consisted of men from various Marine groups who had little time to get acquainted or become familiar with each other's habits and idiosyncrasies.

The battalion was rushed by train to Hampton Roads, Virginia, into makeshift quarters, to await the arrivals of the battleships *Wyoming* and *Arkansas,* which were to become its new home.

The reason for the hurried change of duty for the various Marine groups was unclear, but it was hinted that once aboard the dreadnoughts, the ships would head for the Far East to deter the Japanese takeover of Manchuria.

The cramped and makeshift quarters the men of the battalion occupied at Hampton Roads left much to be desired. We were herded together, slept in makeshift beds, and lived out of our sea bags. This situation, as it affected men who had not had the opportunity to become acquainted, created short tempers.

This was the situation when the Marine next to me, a quiet, introverted individual, sat on his cot shining his shoes. While he sat busy at his task, a red-headed, red-faced Marine from across the room, walked over, appropriated his Kiwi shoe polish, and walked off with it.

"I didn't give you permission to walk off with my shoe polish," the quiet Marine called out.

"I don't need your permission," the red-headed Marine said.

Without uttering another word, the quiet Marine drew the bayonet from its scabbard and headed for the red-faced Marine, whose face had suddenly turned white.

As the irate Marine was about to pass by me, I grasped the bayonet by the blade and held it in a firm grip. "Don't," I cautioned.

For the moment, the men in the room held their collective breath. But it was that moment of reflection that caused the irate Marine to think of the consequences of his act. He released his grip on the hilt of the bayonet and walked back to his cot. Had he pulled the bayonet by the hilt out of my grasp, he would have cut my fingers off.

It wasn't until the following day that the quiet Marine came over to me and said, simply, "Thanks, friend." Thereafter, he would always address me as friend.

A Marine Remembers

The Perplexed Marine

Shortly after being sworn into the Marine Corps in July of 1930, we recruits were ushered into the base auditorium and shown pictures on a movie screen depicting the effects of syphilis on those unfortunate enough to be afflicted with the dreaded disease. And they weren't pretty pictures.

The pictures were of men, women and children. The men and women were covered with red blotches from head to toe. The children, having inherited the disease, were blind. These pictures would haunt me for a long time.

Syphilis, I reasoned, was worse than leprosy. For if the affected parts of a leper's body numbed, the affected parts of a syphilitic's body were alive and well enough to cause the afflicted person unbearable suffering.

The time would come, I thought, when the need for sexual gratification would present itself. What would I do? What should I do? Especially when it came to whores. Would I remember the adage drilled into us by the officer who had shown the blown-up pictures: that as there is no such thing as an unloaded weapon, there is no such thing as an uninfected whore?

Such a time came in Galveston, Texas, where my ship, the USS *Wyoming*, was sent, the Marines to participate in the city's Mardi Gras parade. After the parade, a Southern Marine ten years my senior, nearing the end of his second enlistment and still a private, induced me to accompany him to the city's red light district. I agreed to go as an observer, not as a participant. "We'll head for the colored section," the Southerner said. I made no objections. I was just along for the ride.

When we reached the black section of the red light district, we passed house after house where women sat by their windows beckoning us in. But none of the beckoners seemed to please the Southerner. And then we reached a house where seated by the window was a most attractive looking young mulatto girl. And she wasn't beckoning. We both stopped as if on command. "She's for me," the Southerner decided. I couldn't help but envy him.

On entering the house, we found ourselves in a living room whose furnishings consisted only of a sofa, two stuffed chairs, a dimly lit overhead lighting fixture, and three wall posters depicting Mardi Gras events.

No sooner had we entered the room when an older black woman appeared as if out of nowhere and approached us. "Which of you wants to be first?" she inquired. I shied back, but my companion spoke up. "I don't want you," he said, "I want the girl seated by the window."

The woman glanced toward the window, as did I. "You can't have her," she said, shaking her head.

"And why the hell not?" the Southerner demanded to know.

"Because she's not working tonight," was

A Marine Remembers

the reply.

"And why the hell not?" he repeated his question.

"She's got the woman's sickness," the woman explained. "Come with me," she encouraged. "I'll show you a good time—the best time you ever had."

Thus placated, the other Marine allowed himself to be led into an adjoining bedroom.

After the two left, not knowing what to do, I stood leaning against a wall while the attractive young woman remained seated by the window, eyeing me curiously. I had just about made up my mind to leave the premises and wait outside, when she left her place by the window and came over to me. "Wouldn't you feel more comfortable sitting on the couch?" she asked.

"I guess maybe so," I agreed.

"Come, I'll sit with you," she offered, taking my hand and leading me to the sofa. Once seated, she said, "You're not at all like him, are you?"

"We're not all of us alike," I said.

We sat facing each other and I realized that she was more beautiful up close than she had looked seated by the window in the dim light. "You belong on a painting," the words left my mouth before I realized what I was saying.

She blushed. "That was a nice thing for you to say," she said, taking my hand and rubbing it against her cheek. "Would you like to have a party with me?" she invited.

"I can't," I said.

She moved closer and our bodies touched. "Why not?" she asked.

"I just can't," I said, and then added untruthfully, "I haven't any money."

"I'll do it for love," she said. "It won't cost you anything."

As there is no such thing as an unloaded weapon, there's no such thing as an uninfected whore. The adage, learned on Parris Island, suddenly set off a warning signal in my head. "I just can't," I said.

"Is there something wrong with me?" the young woman asked.

"Oh no," I protested. "I think you're beautiful."

"Is there something wrong with you?" she asked, looking at me quizzically.

I knew what she was inferring. I had said we're not all of us alike. She thought I was queer. "Why does an attractive girl like you have to be in a place like this?" I asked, trying to change the subject.

Suddenly, I realized I had said the wrong thing, and just as suddenly, the girl's face hardened.

She looked away from me, our bodies no longer touching. "Why does an attractive girl like me have to be in a place like this," she said softly, as if to herself. Then, facing me, she said sardonically, "If an attractive girl like me wasn't in a place like this, she would have to be a servant in a Southern household where the men of the

A Marine Remembers

house would fuck her whenever they got the urge and there wouldn't be anything she could do about it. Does that answer your question?"

My face reddened.

"Why are you blushing?" she wanted to know.

"I've never heard a lady use such a word before," I said.

"Did you say lady?" she questioned. Only white women were called ladies. Colored women were called girls no matter how old they were. Before I could reply, she put her arms about me, kissed and embraced me, lay down on the sofa and pulled me on top of her. Her actions were so sudden, they took place before I knew what was happening. Just then, the other Marine and the older woman emerged from the adjoining bedroom, both looking disgruntled.

What happened next would have taxed the ability of a Hollywood screen writer.

I was pushed aside and found myself lying on the floor.

The Southerner, claiming that the young woman had been his first choice, pounced on top of her before she could get off the sofa.

The older woman pounded him with her fists, screaming curses at him as the girl tried to free herself from his grasp, but to no avail. He wouldn't let go of her.

I got off the floor and pulled my companion off the girl, who disappeared from the room as soon as she was free.

The older woman had gone to the kitchen

and now she emerged with a broom, threatening to use it on us if we did not leave the premises.

The Southern Marine refused to leave until he got his money back, claiming that he had been cheated because he had not gotten what he wanted.

The older woman screamed that he had gotten his money's worth and began beating him over the head with the broom, threatening to call the police if he didn't leave her house.

At the mention of police, he decided to leave. I followed close behind. The older woman stationed herself in the doorway, broom in hand.

It would be a long time before I consented to accompany anyone else to a house of prostitution, I decided.

The Major General

Upon my transfer from Parris Island to Quantico, I found myself under the command of the most fearless, the most decorated, the most famous general of the time. Before leaving Quantico to go to sea, I would bear witness to the general's fall from grace, his pending court martial and, finally, his retirement from the Marine Corps.

The country was in the depths of the Depression and all military units suffered as a consequence. Nevertheless, Quantico was a model military facility. Governors, congressmen, ap-

A Marine Remembers

pointed officials, and other dignitaries came to look, inspect, and admire the base.

The streets were paved, curbed, and clean. There was an auditorium which could be converted into a movie theater, a basketball court, or an arena. The facility even had a Hostess House where visitors of note could spend a night in comfort. Although the Marine Corps did not own a single plane, the base boasted an air field.

All of these amenities were made possible through the efforts of one man, Major General Smedley D. Butler, holder of two Congressional Medals of Honor and by far the most famous Marine in the Corps' proud history.

At a time when most people didn't know the name of the Vice President of the United States, they knew who Smedley Butler was. He was a fearless Marine, a Marine's Marine.

But if the general had his strengths, he also had his failings. And they proved to be his undoing. His first failing was that he wasn't a graduate of Annapolis, having been appointed 2nd lieutenant by President McKinley at the age of eighteen during the war with Spain. This failing put him at odds with the Navy hierarchy and was instrumental in his not being appointed commandant, although he was the senior major general in the Corps. A second failing was his lack of diplomacy.

General Butler was the scion of an old Philadelphia family. The Biddles and the Pinchots were not strangers to him. He was a much-sought-after speaker and his speeches received wide coverage. At a time in the nation's history when there was little to stimulate the press, General Butler's rhetoric made good copy.

He addressed the newly arrived at Quantico, stating, "Marines are not afraid of man or the devil." And indeed he wasn't. After he called Benito Mussolini a hit-and-run driver and a liar (the Italian dictator had denied the report that his car had run over and crushed a child and that he had declined to offer assistance, saying, "What is one life in the affairs of a State?"), Butler was recommended for court martial when he refused to apologize to the Italian government.

Finally, having been denied the promotion to major general commandant, he chose to retire and, as he put it, "pursue another line of endeavor." He was in his early fifties—comparatively young as generals go.

His final request of his men was that as they passed the reviewing stand during his farewell parade they sing, "Long, Long Trail." But few of them complied. Most of the men didn't know the words to the song.

The Private and the General

Having been transferred from Parris Island to Quantico, I was assigned guard duty and my post included the quarters in which the

A Marine Remembers

commanding general resided.

The commanding general, holder of two Congressional Medals of Honor, was a well known figure on the national scene who stood in fear of no one. And he was a fearsome figure. Majors quaked before him in the same way that PFC's quaked before majors.

So it was with some trepidation that I, a lowly private, patrolled the area assigned me. I knew the general by sight, had saluted him at various times when we were within saluting distance, but had no wish to encounter him on a one-to-one basis at close range. So each time I neared his quarters, I offered a silent prayer that he would be asleep in bed as all generals should be at this time of night.

My first hour of walking post passed without incident. The night was cool, the stars were out, and there was a rustle through the trees. I felt seven feet tall and congratulated myself on belonging to a proud organization with a proud history, and that at this very moment I was walking in the reflected glory of the famous man whose very name exemplified all that the Marine Corps stood for. So I continued to walk my post, my head held high.

But suddenly, my self-assurance deserted me. Suddenly, I no longer felt seven feet tall. In making my turn some distance from the general's quarters, I saw him standing on the verandah of his house. There was no mistaking the figure. In spite of the coolness of the night, beads of perspiration broke out on my forehead.

There the general stood, bareheaded, wearing pajamas, robe, and slippers, and leaning against the porch railing. And he was staring directly at me.

For a moment, I stood rooted in place trying to decide what to do. To continue forward would mean coming into direct contact with General Smedley D. Butler. But to turn about and retreat would constitute an act of cowardice the general was not likely to overlook.

I prayed that he would return to his quarters. But he was not about to accommodate me. Instead, he remained there staring in my direction as if daring me to stop walking my post. I could feel his eyes boring into me.

Afraid as I was to continue forward, I was even more afraid not to. So, taking a deep breath and offering a silent prayer, I continued forward.

When I reached within saluting distance I halted, faced in his direction, and presented arms. The general, being uncovered, didn't return my salute. (In the Marine Corps, as in the Navy, servicemen who are bareheaded do not salute.)

I came to port arms, then right shoulder arms, and was about to continue walking my post, when the general ordered, "As you were."

I froze in place.

"State your general orders," the general commanded.

Without hesitation, I responded: "To take charge of this post and all government property in view. To walk my post in a military manner, keeping always on the alert and observing everything that takes place within sight and hearing. To give the alarm in case of fire and disorder. To…"

"That's enough," the general said.

I stood frozen in place facing him, but would rather have looked directly into the sun. Then the general's expression softened. "Walk your post, son," he commanded.

I came to present arms, then to port arms, then to right shoulder arms, made an about face, and continued to walk my post.

The Amateur Boxer and the Street Fighter

It had been three months since my transfer from Parris Island to the Quantico Signal Battalion. I was doing my laundry in the basement of the barracks when the invitation came.

"What do you say," the other man asked, "wanna go a couple of rounds with me? I was here the other night when you were going a couple of rounds with your friends."

It was true. Several nights before I had put on the gloves with my best friend, who was some four inches taller than I, and had inadvertently punched him so hard in the midsection that he had trouble catching his breath, which gave us both a scare. That same night, a tall Southerner had asked me to put on the gloves. We sparred for a round and the Southerner swore that when I connected with his jaw he saw stars he never knew existed.

And now this invitation. I knew the Marine who offered it was a club fighter, but I had an idea I could hold my own with him, so I agreed. We put on the boxing gloves that were always available in the basement and squared off. Fortunately for me, there were no witnesses in the basement to record what happened next.

In the first round, the club fighter made me seem inept. He jabbed me at will wherever he had a will to jab and I, a street fighter, had no defense against him. When I tried to rush him his left arm kept me at a distance. At the end of the round, I hadn't gotten close enough to lay a glove on him.

The second round was a replay of the first. This time, however, the club fighter put a little more steam into his punches, hoping that I would quit. I kept thinking, just one punch, just one punch to his midsection, and the tide would turn. But I couldn't deliver that punch. I couldn't get through his defenses. At the end of the second round, the club fighter, barely breathing hard, asked, "Wanna continue?"

I nodded. I still hoped to get my one punch into his midsection.

The third round wasn't much different from the first two. I tried in vain to get under his guard and let go at his midsection. He continued peppering away at me at will and there seemed no way to stop him.

Finally, during the fourth round, the club

fighter stepped back and began unlacing his gloves with his teeth. "I've had enough," he said.

"If that's the way you feel," I agreed, unlacing my own gloves. During the entire bout, I had not managed to land one meaningful blow.

The Family

In the fall of 1930, Major General Smedley D. Butler, commander of the Marine Barracks, Quantico, Virginia, told his men that if the Quantico-based football team defeated the Baltimore firemen football team in their annual football game the following Saturday, all Marines attending would be granted seventy-two hours' leave.

On the Saturday in question, some five hundred Marines entrained at Quantico and debarked seventy-five miles north in Baltimore. We marched in formation to the football field, saw our team defeat the firemen, and then we scattered throughout the city or to our homes, if home was close enough to allow for a return to Quantico Tuesday morning.

It was late Saturday afternoon when the game ended, and I was in a quandary. Having no affiliations with anyone in Baltimore, the question was whether to return to base or hitchhike to New York to visit my family. The weather was cold and wet. Back at the base I would be well-fed, well-housed, and free to spend my time as I wished. What would await me in New York?

My family had dispersed. My oldest brother was married, had a family, lived in the Bronx, and was, to all intents and purposes, divorced from the rest of us. My next older brother was married, had a family, lived somewhere on Long Island, and was also divorced from us. My third older brother had left home years before and had disappeared. No one knew his whereabouts. My oldest sister had left home shortly after the family's arrival in America and resided with our aunt somewhere in the Bronx. My mother had been institutionalized since my enlistment in the Marine Corps. I did not know where she was, except that she was somewhere in the Borough of Queens. The only family members remaining at home were my father and a sister who was two years (or so it was said) older than I. Aside from my mother, I had an affinity with none of them. They might as well have been strangers. But I decided to give it a try, if only to find out my mother's whereabouts and visit with her.

When I arrived in New York Saturday night, it was too late to go knocking at my father's door, so I decided to wait until the following morning. After making a few inquiries, I was directed to an Army and Navy service center located on Park Avenue and 34th Street, where for fifty cents I got a night's lodging.

The following morning, I made my way to

A Marine Remembers

my father's house. My father wasn't at home but my sister was. When she opened the door, she wasn't especially glad to see me. Instead, she continued with the task of polishing her nails, which she had been doing before my arrival. When I asked her to go for a walk with me, she demurred, saying that it wouldn't be seemly. People might talk. So after spending a little time with her, and determining where our mother was institutionalized, I left and went to visit with my mother.

When I arrived at the institution, my mother recognized me and seemed happy to see me. I kissed her on the cheek, visited with her until visiting hours were over, and left, never to see her again.

It was late Sunday night when I returned to New York. Darkness had set in. It was cold and had started to drizzle. Not wanting to return to my father's house, I made my way to Times Square, had a bite to eat at the Automat, and sat there trying to decide what to do. It was too late at night to try to hitch back to Quantico. It being Sunday night, there was only a very slim chance of my getting a ride, so I decided to return to the Army and Navy center to get another night's lodging.

When I left the Army and Navy facility Monday morning, I had exactly twenty cents left in my pocket—just four nickels. I was making my way to Canal Street and the west end of the Holland Tunnel, where I would begin my trek back to Quantico. I was cold, hungry, and almost destitute, when a thought struck me.

Years before, my oldest brother had given me a job clerking in his grocery store. It was in the Bronx, just a block or two from his residence. I remembered that his domineering wife had programmed him to come home for lunch every day at exactly twelve o'clock, no matter what. Since then, after an argument with his then-partner, he had given up the grocery store and had gone into the wholesale egg business on Greenwich Street, just a few blocks from Canal Street. If I hurried and got to his place of business by twelve o'clock, perhaps he would ask me to join him at the appointed hour. When I got to Greenwich Street, I inquired of some of the other wholesale egg dealers, who gave me directions. I made it with fifteen minutes to spare.

I found my brother busily candling (grading) eggs. He looked up, spoke a word of greeting, and continued at his task. I stood by him watching, deftly stepping out of his way when he passed me to displace a case of eggs. He hardly said a word. The minutes were ticking away and I believed that at any moment he would break for lunch and invite me to join him. But nothing of the sort happened. He kept glancing at his watch, glancing at me, and continued with what he was doing. Finally, having decided that an invitation for lunch was not forthcoming, I left, after saying a perfunctory goodbye, and continued on to Canal Street and the Holland Tunnel, the unspent four nickels still in my pocket. On my way to Canal Street, I spent one of my nickels for a cup of coffee. The other fifteen cents, I decided, would be held in reserve until such a time as they were absolutely needed.

It was one in the afternoon when I got to the entrance to the Holland Tunnel and stood on the adjoining sidewalk. I was cold, wet, and hungry when the cop directing traffic into the tunnel saw me standing there and approached me. "Where you headed for?" he asked.

"Quantico," I replied.
"Where's that?" the cop asked.
"Near Washington, D.C.," I said.

The cop stopped the next car headed for the tunnel. "Where you headed for?" he asked the driver. "Philadelphia," was the reply. The cop motioned for me to get in without asking the driver's permission. "This'll take you part of the way," he said.

It wasn't until I reached Washington that I allowed myself to spend two of my three nickels for a doughnut and coffee. When I arrived at Quantico late Monday night, I still had one nickel left.

The Blessing in Disguise

The year was 1932 and my ship, the USS *Arkansas*, was ordered to San Francisco so that our battalion could participate in the George

Washington Birthday Parade. I had never been to the city made famous (and almost destroyed) by its 1906 earthquake. (A year later, I would bear witness to another earthquake—this one in Long Beach—where that city, too, was almost totally destroyed.)

The battalion of Marines marched down Market Street with a six-foot three-inch major at its head, his officers behind him, and the troops behind the officers, making a spectacular showing. We were applauded by the people lining the sidewalks as well as by people leaning out of their windows from buildings along the route.

When the parade was over the Marines were granted liberty. I decided to go see a movie featuring Ralph Bellamy. After leaving the movie theater, I strolled down Market Street rubbernecking. Feeling uncomfortably warm, I undid the top two hooks of my uniform collar. No sooner had I done so when I espied the major walking towards me from the opposite direction. I knew that by unhooking the top two hooks of my uniform jacket I was considered out of uniform, but, not wishing to call the major's attention to that fact by raising my arms to my collar to secure the hooks, I decided to leave well enough alone and hope the major wouldn't notice.

When we came within saluting distance, I saluted the major, a salute the major returned. "Are you having a good time?" the major asked, feigning not to notice my unhooked collar.

A Marine Remembers

"Yes, sir," I replied.

"Well, continue on your way," the major said.

"Thank you, sir," I replied, as I again saluted.

We parted company. Nothing more was said of the incident.

Several weeks later, the USS *Arkansas* back in its home port of Long Beach, the battalion stood troop inspection. I was in the front rank and my friend, Charlie Kusheba, stood alongside me. When the major stepped in front of Charlie, the latter, as was customary, threw up his rifle to the port arms position, opened the bolt, quickly glanced down and up, as was customary to make sure it wasn't loaded, and held it in front of him for inspection. The major grabbed the rifle from him, turned it every which way, lifted it up to glance down the barrel, handed it back to him, and asked, "How many lands and grooves in your rifle?"

My friend's face turned red.

"Well?" the major questioned.

"I don't know, sir," he had to admit.

The major turned to the first sergeant who was behind and to the right of him. "This man doesn't belong in the Marine Corps," he said. "We'll have to do something about that."

And then he stepped in front of me.

"Good God," I thought, "he's going to ask me the same question and I don't know how many fucking lands and grooves are in a rifle either."

As my friend had done, I threw my rifle to the port position, opened the bolt, quickly glanced up and down, and held it for the major to inspect, my knees shaking.

"And you," the major said. "Next time I see you on the street out of uniform I'll see to it that you never leave this ship again." Then he stepped to the Marine alongside me.

That same day, after troop inspection, there wasn't a Marine aboard ship who didn't know how many lands and grooves were in his rifle.

The Earthquake

I was standing a radio watch aboard the USS *Arkansas* anchored in Long Beach Harbor, then the home of the Pacific Fleet. The radio room, situated a deck below the water line, was manned by Navy personnel, but two Marine radiomen were assigned to stand watch with them and I was one of the two. The weather was pleasantly cool topside, but inside the radio room it was uncomfortably warm, so, as was permitted under the circumstances, I had on only socks, shoes, trousers, and a skivvy shirt.

There was little radio traffic going on, since the ships in the harbor communicated visually by semaphore or blinker.

With little radio activity, I sat at my station with headphones on my head, an Underwood typewriter in front of me, and a ra-

A Marine Remembers

dio log sheet inserted in the typewriter. To stay alert I drank cup after cup of Joe—a staple available in all radio rooms at all times. As was required, I periodically typed "no signals" on the radio log sheet to indicate that none were being transmitted over the airwaves.

"Anything happening?" the supervisor, a radioman 1st class, asked on entering the radio room.

"Like Sunday on a farm," I replied.

No sooner had I spoken than the ship began to vibrate. Soon, the thirty thousand-ton battleship was rattling and rolling to such a degree and with such noises that she seemed to be coming apart at the seams. It was as if she were about to be torn asunder.

Nobody knew what was happening. Men in all states of undress began running topside, wanting to abandon what they thought was a sinking ship.

I sat glued to my chair, scared out of my wits, unable to leave my post, fully expecting the Pacific Ocean to break the ship's seams and engulf us.

Then, after what seemed an interminable length of time, the vibration and noise stopped. Before I had time to recover from the shock, all Marines aboard ship were ordered ashore on the double, and I was immediately relieved of my watch.

Rushing to my compartment, I had time only to grab my cap, overcoat, rifle, belt, and bayonet and hurry topside where motor launches were already standing by to take the Marines to the beach.

Within the hour, a fellow Marine and I were posted in an alley between a YMCA building and a Post Office, guarding a registered mail truck that had been buried under a pile of bricks caused by a collapsed chimney on the YMCA building.

The Power of the Bayonet

The Pacific Fleet had left, but my ship, the USS *Arkansas*, and its battalion of Marines remained behind to patrol the streets of Long Beach. We would be doing so for the next thirty days.

It seemed to me that no building had been left untouched. Some private dwellings had even moved off their foundations.

Our orders were short and to the point: prevent looters from entering the city, prevent looting inside the city, and prevent people from entering buildings we considered to be unsafe. Aftershocks were occurring quite frequently and falling debris posed a danger to everyone in or near those buildings. We carried out our orders diligently.

Another Marine and I were on patrol when a group of women approached us with a complaint. They told us that a neighborhood store had increased its prices to such an extent that they could no longer afford to buy what

A Marine Remembers

they needed. Although we had received no orders pertaining to price gouging, I told the other Marine, "Let's go and take a look."

When we reached the store in question, I told the other Marine to wait outside while I went in. Inside the store, I saw two women arguing with the proprietor and heard him shout, "Take it or leave it." Without making my presence felt, I walked out of the place and told the other Marine what was happening.

"Let's look the place over for structural damage," the other Marine suggested.

"Good idea," I agreed.

We gazed up at the roof of the one-story building, noticed a few overhanging eaves at the front entrance, and decided that the store was unsafe for occupation.

With the other Marine stationed outside to prevent people from entering, I returned inside, announced that the building was unsafe, and ushered the customers out. The proprietor ran after me cursing and screaming, but I paid no attention to him. He threatened me, but to no avail. Outside, we stood guard, preventing anyone from entering.

All of a sudden, the proprietor—a short, balding, middle-aged man—ran out of the place to go and look for a higher authority to countermand our decision. He was gone almost half an hour, but returned with a Marine lieutenant in tow.

"What's the problem?" the lieutenant wanted to know.

We pointed to the overhanging eaves at the front entrance to the store. He looked up, a dubious expression on his face. I then advised the officer of the numerous complaints we had received about price gouging.

"This store will remain closed," he told the proprietor. Then, turning to the two of us, he added, "Pass that order along to your reliefs."

The Tidal Wave

He was termed "The Philosopher" and was possibly the oldest PFC in the history of the Marine Corps. He had taken part in the Argonne offensive, had served in China in the early twenties after the Boxer Rebellion, and had done duty in every "banana republic" where Marines were stationed.

He hadn't always been a PFC. At one time or another he had held every enlisted man's rating available. But he had been busted back to PFC. Finally, he and the Marine Corps hierarchy reached an unspoken and unwritten agreement. He would be allowed to stay in the Corps if he did not seek any further promotions.

His weakness was beer. He had been left behind at Hampton Roads because he had imbibed too much of it and had to be checked into the Naval hospital and held for observation. He had often said that when it came time to meet his Maker, he would like to meet Him inside a

A Marine Remembers

keg of beer.

And he said other things. And when he spoke, those around him listened. One of the things he said was that in times of havoc and upheaval, the general populace always flocked to the man in uniform, be that the uniform of a Marine, a policeman, a postman, or a boy scout. He recommended that every family keep some kind of uniform in its closet for emergency purposes to be used, in times of distress, for a pacifier or security blanket. And he proved to be right.

The third day following the earthquake, while he was patrolling the streets of Long Beach with fixed bayonet, women of all ages who would have, under ordinary circumstances, not given him the time of day, attached themselves to him. They brought him sandwiches and lemonade and coffee and asked questions. One of their most frequent questions was, "Is there going to be a tidal wave?" Never having heard the term before, his stock answer was: "Do I look worried?"

But he was curious, so the next time a Marine sentry crossed his path, he asked, "What's a tidal wave?"

"Damned if I know," was the answer.

He continued walking his post and when he came into contact with another Marine sentry, he asked, "What's a tidal wave?"

"Beats me," was the reply.

Then he met a sailor on his way back to his ship. If anyone would know about tidal waves, he thought, a sailor should. "What's a tidal wave?" he asked.

"I think it has something to do with the tide and waves," was the reply.

It wasn't until after he met the man he called "friend"— the Marine who had grasped his bayonet at Hampton Roads—me—that he learned what a tidal wave was.

That's when he began looking worried.

The Ensign

The first time I had knowledge of Ensign Giles, it was not under the most favorable circumstances.

It was the morning after an overnight liberty. I was hurrying back to my ship, intent on catching the last motor launch leaving the dock for the USS *Arkansas,* when I saw an Italian Marine, a member of my unit, sitting on the curb with his head in his hands. The son of a bitch has done it again, I thought. My first impulse was to let him sit there, miss the motor launch, and face the consequences. I had played the role of Good Samaritan before and gotten no thanks for it.

In Panama City I had accompanied him to a whorehouse and when, after half an hour of trying, the inebriated Marine wasn't able to function, and the whore insisted he leave, he wouldn't leave without getting his money back. The whore called the Panamanian police and

A Marine Remembers

we ran back to the ship with the police chasing us all the way.

And then there was Seattle. I literally had to fight him to get him back to the ship after an overnight liberty, got mauled in the process, and wound up with a bump on my head.

But how could I just leave him sitting there? Marines didn't abandon other Marines when they were in trouble. "Up on your feet," I ordered as I approached him. "Go to hell," was the response.

Again I wanted to leave him sitting there and again my better instincts prevented me from doing so. I lifted him to his feet where he stood swaying, and half carried him to where the motor launch was, my charge fighting me all the way. The motor launch was about to pull away when the coxswain saw us coming and waited for us to board.

Once the motor launch reached the ship, all the passengers scrambled up the gangplank and stood aside to see what would happen. I pushed my charge up the gangway ahead of me where, after reaching the deck, he attempted a half-hearted salute and mumbled a request for permission to come aboard.

Ensign Giles, the officer of the deck, looked the dark-complexioned Italian Marine up and down, noted his unhooked collar, the trace of vomit on his uniform jacket, and askew cap and sneeringly said, "I didn't know they allowed niggers in the Marine Corps."

"Who're you calling a nigger, you son of

a bitch," the Italian Marine wanted to know, and attempted to take a swing at the officer of the deck, a swing the officer had no trouble avoiding.

A couple of other Marines and I hurriedly ran the Italian Marine down to our quarters, trying to avoid further trouble. But everyone thought that it was all over for him. Taking a swing at an officer was a general court martial offense and it was feared that he would spend the next twenty years at Leavenworth.

But, oddly enough, nothing more came of the incident. Ensign Giles's reputation was so bad that he chose not to report the incident or if he did, it was decided that, considering his own behavior at the time, no action was required.

The second time I came into contact with Ensign Giles was when I was doing sentry duty aboard ship while at sea.

Why they needed a sentry to guard a prisoner safely locked behind prison bars was beyond my understanding. There was no way the prisoner could escape, and if such an unlikely event occurred, there was no place for him to escape to. But mine was not to reason why, so I sat outside the brig reading while the prisoner was inside the brig sleeping.

I had the 1200 to 0400 watch and it was nearing 0200. I was sitting there, unarmed, listening to the prisoner snore, when Ensign Giles, then the officer of the deck, made his appearance accompanied by the master at arms, a chief

A Marine Remembers

boatswain's mate.

I put my book aside and got to my feet. The ensign eyed me up and down disdainfully for a moment and said, "Make believe the prisoner has a gun, points it at you, and orders you to open the cell door, what would you do?"

"In that case," I replied, "I'd take my own gun out and shoot him."

"But you haven't got a gun," the ensign said.

"Sir," I replied, "if I'm going to make believe the prisoner has a gun, then I'll make believe that I have one too." Nothing came of that incident either. It was well established aboard ship that the ensign was an undesirable, that he was looked down on by both officers and enlisted men, and that if it weren't that his father was captain of the flagship USS *Pennsylvania,* his transfer would have been assured.

As it turned out, Ensign Giles became my biggest booster. It was during the time I was standing radio watches and the ensign was appointed radio officer.

Ensign Giles didn't know Morse code or radio procedure and each time he plugged a spare headset into a radio receiver the man on watch, not wanting to be blamed for the result, hung up his own headset, walked away, and left him sitting there alone.

I was the only exception. Feeling somewhat sorry for the ensign's plight, I not only allowed him to sit by me and listen in, but over a period of time taught him Morse code as well as

Navy procedure. Ensign Giles was so grateful that he asked if there was anything he could do for me.

"Yes," I replied, "get me a PFC rating."

After more than two years in the Marine Corps, and although my job as a radio operator called for it, I couldn't make PFC. There just weren't any vacancies available.

Ensign Giles tried every which way, pulled every string, even contacted his father, captain of the USS *Pennsylvania*, flagship of the Pacific Fleet, but to no avail. My battalion's complement didn't call for it.

A Penny Saved is a Penny Lost

The pay of a private in the Marine Corps when I enlisted in 1930 was $21 a month, minus twenty cents given to the Navy for medical care and hospitalization. (The Marine Corps does not have its own medical facilities. All doctors and corpsmen are Navy personnel. The chaplains, who are also Navy personnel, are provided free of charge.)

When President Roosevelt came into office, he cut the salaries of all government employees by fifteen percent. Since members of the armed forces were government employees, they were affected by the fifteen percent cut. This reduced a private's pay to seventeen dollars and sixty-five cents a month, payable at the end of the month. While I was serving at the mess hall,

A Marine Remembers

the cost of all broken dishes and lost or stolen silverware was deducted from my pay.

For a private in the Marine Corps to save part of his monthly pay after purchasing toilet articles and articles needed for the care and maintenance of his equipment and other necessities, he would have to abstain from drinking, smoking, contact with the opposite sex, and limit his consumption of Milky Ways. But I decided to give it a try.

I didn't trust myself to keep the money I had saved on my person. I didn't want to have physical contact with it. So I decided to open a savings account far from where I was stationed, so it would not be within easy reach. As I was stationed aboard ship on the West Coast, reason dictated that I select a bank on the East Coast.

With that in mind, I chose The Franklin National Bank ("A penny saved is a penny earned"), located at 1111 Connecticut Avenue N.W., Washington, D.C, and made out an allotment payable directly to them in the sum of ten dollars a month. After accumulating the princely amount of forty dollars over a period of four months, my wish was realized. I never made physical contact with it.

On April 16, 1933, I received a communication from that worthy institution which read in part, "We advise that this bank did not receive a license to reopen after the Bank Holiday and funds on deposit cannot be withdrawn from the bank."

At a nickel each, the forty dollars would have purchased 800 Milky Ways.

The Coal Miner and the East-Sider

It was January, 1934 and "C" Battery, 10th Marines, stationed at Quantico, Virginia, had just returned from its morning exercises. After changing from their dungarees to their winter greens, the men, singly and in pairs, left the squad room and made their way to the mess hall for noonday chow. Only a husky coal miner and I remained behind, both of us busily engaged in shining our shoes and fair leather belts.

"Coming?" the coal miner asked. He had finished first.

"Wait a minute," I replied. "Afraid you'll go hungry?"

The coal miner walked over to me and punched me playfully in the stomach. "Get the lead out," he said.

I, the East-Sider, just as playfully, punched him back, saying, "Hold your water. You won't go hungry."

The coal miner punched my stomach a little more forcefully and I returned the compliment just as forcefully.

And then it happened. Without another word, as if by mutual agreement, we two Marines walked to the center of the squad room, the two rows of bunks aligned on either side of us, braced ourselves, and with feet wide apart, and without apparent reason, began to punch each other in the midsection with all the force at our command. Neither of us stepped back or uttered a word as we continued the test of endurance.

Fortunately for both of us, the first sergeant happened to be passing by and looked into the squad room. "Knock off the skylarking or I'll put you both on report," he ordered.

So we knocked off the skylarking. Without admitting it to ourselves or each other, we were both grateful to the first sergeant.

The silent test of endurance was over and we were both able to save face. We finished dressing, walked to the mess hall together, each of us painfully aware of his tender midsection, and neither of us ever mentioned the incident again.

The Ham Sandwich

It was a gala affair. There were more than a hundred people present, mostly relatives, who had come from all over the country for the occasion. In a sense, it was a gathering of the clan, some of whom had never met before.

The wedding was being held in the garden of a posh hotel. Twelve rows of white folding chairs were arranged, five on each side of the bridal path. That way, all seated would be able to see the bride and groom as they made their way down the aisle.

Samuel Rimler

A not-so-special invited guest, I was seated on a chair in the last row farthest away from the bride and groom. The woman seated next to me was not my wife. Because we had arrived late, my wife and I had been unable to get adjoining seats.

I gazed about as I always did in the midst of a gathering. I knew for sure there was one person there older than me. As for the rest of the assemblage, it looked like I was the oldest.

As I generally did when trying to judge the ages of people, I associated them with presidential administrations. I was from the Roosevelt era. The others seemed to go back no farther than Eisenhower.

All chitchat subsided as the rabbi, clearing his throat, made ready to speak. "We are gathered together," he began, "to join and make as one these two beautiful people. In this vast universe of ours, and more especially on this planet earth with its more than five billion inhabitants, the odds against these two people meeting were incomprehensible. Yet they met. What caused this miracle to happen? What brought them together?"

"A ham sandwich," I muttered.

"Ssshhh," the woman seated next to me cautioned. "The food'll come later. And they don't serve ham at Jewish weddings."

I looked at her without seeing her. Then I turned away from her and listened to the rabbi talk without hearing him. My thoughts began to wander.

A Marine Remembers

It was 1934 and I was back in the Marine Corps stationed at Quantico, Virginia. I was twenty-two years old and it was the month of my birth. I was never really sure what day in April I was born so I'd opted for the 15th, the middle of the month. The Marine Corps had accepted that date although I could produce no birth certificate to bear it out.

I liked the Marine Corps. The Corps had given me a home, food, clothing, and spending money. I had fully expected to make it my career.

I was what was termed a thirty-year man. Having enlisted in July of 1930, I had twenty-six years and three months to go.

My thoughts continued to wander. I was back aboard the USS *Argonne*, a member of "C" Battery, 10th Marines. "C" Battery, 10th Marines, an elite unit stationed at Quantico, Virginia, had been selected to participate in joint Army and Marine Corps exercises at Guantanamo Bay, Cuba. There would be observers of high rank from both services watching and grading us. The landings were to be made the following morning and the battery commander was briefing us while the ship was still at sea.

"It is of the utmost importance that we take possession of the area assigned us in the shortest possible time," he was saying, and focusing his eyes on his radio operator, me, added, "it is especially important that we establish radio communications with the command ship anchored in the harbor in the shortest possible time. We all know what we have to do. Let's do it. Let's show the bastards how it's done."

At 0700 the morning of the landing, we were fed a breakfast of hard boiled eggs, toast, and coffee and given a cheese sandwich and a ham sandwich to take with us. At 0800 we were climbing down the cargo nets of the ship, anchored three hundred yards off shore, into the ship's motor launches. By 0830, because of the high seas, most of the hard boiled eggs and toast had been returned gratuitously and by 0845 we hit the beaches.

I jumped over the gunwale of the motor launch into water up to my chest, holding my equipment above my head, and fought my way to the beach. Once ashore, three other Marines and I began our climb up hill 250 on top of which I would set up my equipment and try to establish radio communications with the command ship anchored in the harbor.

It was an almost impossible task. The brush was dry and the going was tough. It was impossible to gain a foothold. I would climb up a step and slide down a step. More than once, I would climb up a step and slide down two. Finally, our uniforms wet with perspiration, the others and I reached the top of the hill. I set up my equipment and established communication with the command ship in the harbor. Then I stood up and watched the panoramic scene below.

A Marine Remembers

The Marines were all in their assigned places, but the soldiers were in trouble. None of them had ever climbed down cargo nets before and a few of them, having fallen into the sea, had to be fished out. Those who had reached shore were wandering around trying to regroup. It was funny but we were too tired to laugh.

We were all soaked with perspiration. We had brought along canteens full of water, but water wasn't a problem. When we reached the top of Hill 250, the locals were waiting for us with cold bottles of Pepsi Cola.

Those who had money paid for those who hadn't and we sat down to chow while awaiting orders. I pulled out my cheese sandwich and ate. I had consumed so many bottles of Pepsi that I had no desire for the ham sandwich and forgot about it.

The other three Marines and I sat on top of the hill the rest of the morning and most of the afternoon, the hot tropical sun beating down on us, drinking Pepsi while awaiting orders. Then, orders finally came: "Cease all present exercises and return to ship. Well done."

Back aboard ship, the battery commander held troop inspection. With the first sergeant a step behind him, notebook in hand, the battery commander walked up and down the ranks of his men inspecting their arms and equipment. When he got to me, he stopped. The first sergeant stopped as well. "This man has an oil stain on the back of his pack," he said, "make a note of it." The first sergeant duly made a note of it.

The battery commander had singled me out. I couldn't believe it. And after what I had done. After breaking my back climbing Hill 250 and establishing radio communications with the Command Ship, for which my unit had received a "Well done" message, I had been reprimanded. And for something I was totally unaware of. I couldn't get it out of my mind.

When my unit was given the order to fall out, I examined my pack. Sure enough, there was an oil stain on the back of it. For a moment I puzzled over the matter. Then I stuck my hand inside the pack and pulled out the ham sandwich I hadn't eaten. The rest was elementary. The sun beating down on me had caused the suet in the ham to melt and stain my pack.

Fifteen minutes after the incident, the entire matter was forgotten. It's doubtful if the first sergeant even made a note of it. But I remembered and it ate at me. And I wanted to get even. But how? How does a private get even with a captain? I puzzled over the matter without coming to a resolution. And then, suddenly, a bright idea occurred to me. I would request a transfer.

Then, just as suddenly, I dismissed the idea. I really didn't want a transfer. I liked the outfit—liked the men in it. In a strange way, I even liked the captain, although he had reprimanded me. But how else could I let him know

A Marine Remembers

how I felt?

I was brooding over the matter when the company clerk approached. "What are you thinking about?" he asked, just to strike up a conversation.

"I was thinking of asking for a transfer," I replied.

"Sure?" he asked.

"Sure."

"Wait 'til we get back to Quantico," he said. "I'll look up your record book and see what the possibilities are."

"I'll appreciate your help," I said, doubtfully. And that is where the matter stood.

When we got back to Quantico, there was so much to do that I had little time to think about it. I was still brooding over the matter, but it no longer seemed as important as it had been. I had about given up all thought of a transfer when the company clerk contacted me. "You enlisted in New York and you're a short timer," he said.

"Well?"

"Are you planning to re-enlist?"

"I haven't decided."

"Well, let me spell it out for you," he said. "The government is always looking to save money. If you're getting out and are discharged here, you'll be entitled to five cents a mile transportation from here to your place of enlistment, roughly fifteen dollars. But if you're discharged in New York, you'll be allowed no transportation, therefore saving the government fifteen dollars. Ergo, your chances of getting a transfer are good."

"Supposing I'm transferred to New York and decide to stay in?"

"That's another matter. But remember, if you get out you'll have ninety days on the outside during which time you can come back in and still be entitled to your shipping over pay. You decide and let me know. If you decide on a transfer, I'll tell you how to go about it."

"I'll let you know," I promised.

Although no allusion by the captain or first sergeant, or anyone else for that matter, had been made regarding the incident aboard ship, I continued to brood over it. If the captain had spoken one kindly word or made one kindly gesture, I would have forgotten about the matter. But the captain didn't so I didn't. The next time I saw the company clerk I told him I wanted the transfer—and I was instructed how to go about requesting one.

But each time I went into the captain's office to request the transfer, my request was denied and I was ordered out of his office. And after each denial, the company clerk told me to go and try again. It became a duel of wits between the company clerk and the captain, with me in the middle.

After the third try and third denial, I was instructed, "This time insist that a letter be written to that effect. According to Navy Regulations, a letter must be written even if he disapproves

A Marine Remembers

it. So make sure that you use the word insist."

So I went back and insisted that a letter be written stating that I was to be transferred to Marine Barracks, Brooklyn Navy Yard. The letter was written. The captain disapproved it. The battalion commander disapproved it. The commanding general Marine Base, Quantico, Virginia, disapproved it. But Washington approved it. The government wanted to save the fifteen dollars transportation.

"You'll be back," the other Marines said when I left the Navy yard. "You'll get hungry and come back."

But I didn't come back. Once outside, I got a job making deliveries. On one of my deliveries, I met a girl. The girl became my wife. Subsequently, we moved to California. My wife had a brother who followed her there. Her brother begat a daughter. His daughter met a boy. Now they were getting married.

The woman sitting next to me looked at me. "Hmmm," she said. "A ham sandwich."

I looked at her. If it weren't for a ham sandwich, you wouldn't be here, I thought. None of us would be here.

The Bridge of Sighs

July 24, 1934 would ever be ingrained in my mind. It might just as well have been tattooed on my chest. It was the date I was discharged from the Marine Corps.

As I left the Marine Barracks at the Brooklyn Navy Yard and headed for the Brooklyn Bridge, I cursed the day pigs were invented.

If I had only eaten that damned ham sandwich while on maneuvers at Guantanamo Bay. Had I eaten it, the incident aboard the USS *Argonne* wouldn't have taken place. I'd still be attached to "C" Battery, 10th Marines, and I would have shipped over. Now, feeling like a pariah, I found myself on the outside looking in.

And as I cursed the pigs for having been born, I cursed myself for getting into this predicament. I could just as easily have overlooked the incident. Everyone else in "C" Battery did. But stupidity, which I mistook for pride, impelled me to insist on a transfer. So now I was going to walk the bridge to give back the nickel the government had allotted me for transportation to my place of enlistment.

As I crossed the bridge, I stopped periodically to look down at the waters below. I didn't want to continue forward. And yet, I was ashamed to turn back.

I could have gone back. My discharge papers read, "Recommended For Reenlistment." But I was ashamed. Before I left, my fellow Marines had taunted, "You'll be back. You'll get hungry and come back." I wanted to prove them wrong. But I knew that the odds were in their favor.

With the country in deep Depression,

A Marine Remembers

with lawyers resorting to ambulance chasing or vying for jobs at the post office, what chance did I have with my meager formal education?

In the Marine Corps, I was a something. I was an expert rifleman. I was adept in radio communications. I was well-liked, well thought of, and had a spotless record. What would become of me on the outside? Would it be like it was before I joined the Corps? Would the jungle reclaim the land?

So I stopped periodically to gaze down at the waters of the East River and sighed. And a deep depression set in—a depression from which I would never fully recover. But I continued forward.

I crossed the Brooklyn Bridge, made my way to Rivington Street, and reached the apartment shared by my father (with whom I had no affinity) and my sister (whose mind was failing)—a vermin-infested apartment where cockroaches landscaped the walls.

The Reunion

"How long have you been in the Marine Corps, corporal?"

"Three years, sir."

"You don't have to sir me," I said. I was a chief but not an officer.

I sat on the passenger side of the jeep. The warden of the Navy prison at Norfolk had discovered that I was on the Navy base and had sent a driver to pick me up. It was September of 1945 and I was on my way from Guantanamo Bay, Cuba to Bainbridge, Maryland, to be separated from the Navy. We were to have lunch at the BOQ (bachelor officers quarters) dining room and spend the afternoon together, after which I would be driven back to my own quarters. The last time we had been together was in November of 1940. At that time, the warden, now a first lieutenant, had been an acting 1st sergeant. Three years prior to that he had been responsible for my having enlisted in the Marine Corps Reserves.

Our wives and we had met at a social affair. The year was 1937, three years after my discharge from the regular Marine Corps. I was wearing my honorable discharge button in the lapel of my jacket, as I always did when dressed in a suit, and he had spotted it. It turned out that he too was an ex-Marine, having been discharged from the service a year before me.

"There aren't too many of us around," he said.

"You're the first one I've met," I agreed.

"Say," he suggested, "we've formed a reserve battalion based at the Brooklyn Navy Yard. How about joining us?"

"Let me think about it," I replied.

I hadn't much use for the reserves. When I was stationed at Quantico a unit of the reserves had arrived at the base for their two-week training course and had occupied the upper floor of the same barracks I was in. They looked and behaved like a sad lot and after they departed, the regulars had to clean up after them. But the other ex-Marine persisted.

"How many ex-Marines do you have in the battalion?" I inquired.

"There's the captain of 'A' Company and myself."

The captain of 'A' Company and myself, I thought. Just two ex-Marines. The others must be of the same caliber as had come to Quantico for their summer training, or vacations, as the regulars had termed it.

"What kind of rating can I expect?" I wanted to know. "And, by the way, what's your rating?"

"I'm a sergeant, acting 1st sergeant. I'll introduce you to the major and we can discuss ratings with him."

After much urging, I agreed to come around and be interviewed by the battalion commander. But although the major was anxious to have me enlist in his outfit, the best he could offer me was a PFC rating. It seemed that when the battalion was formed, all ratings had been assigned on a first come, first served basis. It took me four years of regular service and two years of reserve duty to achieve the rating of the corporal who was now driving me to have lunch with the warden.

Samuel Rimler

The Pitiless Sea

    I stood topside of the four-stack destroyer grasping the lifeline and I was scared.

    The World War I craft was of the Calhoun class. Two of them had been assigned to transport my battalion to Guantanamo Bay. Fifty would be turned over to the British as part of Lend Lease.

    We were crossing the Caribbean in the midst of a hurricane. And it was a frightening experience. I had never seen the sea in such a rage. The craft was rolling and pitching and when she rolled to the starboard side where I was standing I could stretch out my hand and touch the angry waves. And then, just as I was sure she was about to capsize on top of me, she rolled to port and I had all I could do to maintain my grip on the lifeline to keep from being tossed to the other side. And, she was awash. The only dry places aboard the ship were inside the compartments from which I had just escaped.

    I had never been seasick, but what went on below in the crowded compartments turned my stomach. The men were packed like sardines in a can. They slept side by side and head to foot with hardly enough space to walk between them. And, worse, the latrines were situated in the midst of them and when they had to urinate or have a bowel movement, their leavings swished back and forth inside the long latrines until they reached either

A Marine Remembers

one or the other end of the receptacle, to be deposited into the sea. And it was continuous. And it made me sick, forcing me topside.

But that was not the only reason I opted to take my chances topside. I was also scared of being trapped in a pocket of air if the ship capsized. I was afraid to die, but more afraid to die a slow death. Many of the others had crosses and St. Christopher medals to console them, but I had none of these. I didn't even have a Star of David medal to succor me, although I didn't consider King David much of a role model. So I remained topside holding on to the lifelines and watching the waves sometimes five feet above me and sometimes five feet below where I stood. I was like a rabbit mesmerized by a snake. I was afraid to stay, but more afraid to leave.

And then something happened to resolve my situation. I was being sought out. My commanding officer, himself deathly seasick, had sent messengers all over the ship to try and locate me and one of them finally found me topside. When I reported to the major, I was told that the radiomen who were standing watches in the radio room were so seasick they could no longer function and that the ship's captain, after making inquiries, had discovered there was a Marine radioman aboard. When I reached the radio room, the captain asked if I had ever stood watch aboard a naval vessel. I replied in the affirmative, stating that I had stood watches on the USS *Wyoming* and USS *Arkansas*. The captain ordered me to take over the watch, which I did.

As it turned out, the two World War I destroyers reached their destination the following morning, delivering their contingents of Marine reserves without incident and in calm seas.

The Arrangement

When I joined the reserve battalion based at the Brooklyn Navy Yard, the only rating I could get was PFC. All of the NCO ratings had been distributed at the time the battalion was organized and its table of organization didn't allow for any more non-commissioned officers.

The term battalion was, to all intents and purposes, a misnomer. It consisted only of "A" Company and Headquarters Company. Even Headquarters Company was a misnomer, since it only consisted of the battalion commander, the sergeant who had recruited me, and the sergeant's brother, who was a corporal affiliated with the Civil Service and who had never been associated with any military organization. As an inducement to enlist, the battalion commander had promised me the first NCO rating available, but could make no promises as to when such an opening would occur.

And yet, although just a PFC, I was accepted into the battalion hierarchy. Because I was friends with the sergeant who had re-

A Marine Remembers

cruited me and with his brother, who was headquarters clerk, and because I was one of only three Marines who had seen service in the regular Marine Corps, I associated with and socialized with the other NCOs and was generally looked up to.

When I finally did make corporal, it was due to another Marine corporal's misfortune.

The battalion was at Sea Girt, New Jersey for its annual two-week training exercises and was at the rifle range firing for record when one of its corporals was caught cheating. He was summarily dismissed from the service. Upon our return to our home base at the Brooklyn Navy Yard, I was promoted to the vacancy. The battalion commander had kept his word. It would be another two years before another promotion would be forthcoming.

In 1940, with war in Europe and Japan threatening, orders were received from Washington to build the battalion to full strength. Other companies were formed and Headquarters Company received additional personnel. With this increase, two ratings were created: sergeant and staff sergeant. The battalion clerk and I were both due for promotion. The question was which of us was entitled to the higher rating. It was a decision the battalion commander had to make, but he had no wish to do so and left it to us to decide.

The battalion clerk, still a corporal, was adept at what he did insofar as office work was concerned, but knew nothing about handling men, drilling them, instructing them, or otherwise dealing with them. I had been in the Marine regulars, was a qualified radio operator, an expert rifleman, and knew how to teach, instruct, and drill the sudden influx of new Marine reserve recruits.

We had become close friends. I knew I could have the staff sergeant's rating for the asking. But I also knew that the battalion clerk hungered for it, especially now that his brother had been promoted to first sergeant. We talked the matter over amicably and I volunteered to accept the lower rating, provided I was given complete control over the men in the company and that under no circumstances would the other attempt to interfere with the way I handled them or with any of their activities. The battalion clerk quickly agreed.

And so it was that I accepted the rank of sergeant while the other was promoted from corporal to staff sergeant, performing the same tasks in the battalion office as he did when he was a corporal.

The Teacher

I gazed around the classroom. The twelve Marine Corps reservists of Headquarters Company seated at their desks were there to learn radio communications and I was there to teach them.

A little over ten years before at Parris Is-

A Marine Remembers

land, I had sat behind such a desk, as attentive as they and as apprehensive, waiting for the instructor to speak. Now at Quantico, I was their sergeant and instructor and they were waiting for me to speak.

"Whether by word of mouth, the written word, the use of hand signals, or other means, there is a need for communication in every facet of our society," I began. "All of these methods are used in the Marine Corps and are elementary. It is another means of communication we are here to learn—radio communication.

"Radio signals travel at the speed of light. This means that if you place your hand on the key in front of you, provided it is attuned to the proper frequency, the man on the moon will be able to pick up your signal almost instantaneously—provided, of course, that there is a man on the moon."

The students burst into laughter, which was all right with me. I wanted them to feel more relaxed.

"You are here," I continued, "to learn International Morse Code. This code consists of four dots and dashes. Depending on how they are arranged, those four dots and dashes cover the entire twenty-six letters of the alphabet. Numerals consist of five dots and dashes, but we will go into that later."

One of the reservists raised his hand.

"Yes, Pauling," I said.

"It is hard to believe that only four dots and dashes can cover the entire alphabet."

"I thought so too until I reminded myself that The Bible in its entirety consists of only twenty-six letters of the alphabet.

Samuel Rimler

"Your desks are equipped with headsets, telegraph keys, paper and pencils," I continued. "For now, forget about the keys. Make believe they aren't there. I am going to start off by sending the first six letters of the alphabet in proper sequence. I will do so six times. Then I'll send those same signals another half dozen times but this time I'll scatter them. I'll continue this process with the next six letters of the alphabet until the entire alphabet is covered, not forgetting the last two letters. Then I'll repeat the entire process from beginning to end. Pick up your pencils and print, I repeat print, the letters as you recognize them. If you make mistakes, do not be concerned. And do not rush. Accuracy is more important than speed. Now, adjust your headsets and let us begin."

With those words I repaired to my desk, placed my fingers on the key attached to the oscillator, and began to transmit as slowly as I could.

At 1600 we had been at it all day, but for a break for noonday chow and a couple of short breaks in the afternoon. And things were going well. There wasn't a man there who had not learned the twenty-six letters of the alphabet in Morse Code. Tomorrow I would take them to the next stages. "Pay close attention to what I'm about to say," I told them. "I'm going to transmit a message in Morse Code and I want all of you to copy it. I will pause a second or two between words so that you can space them. I want you to copy this message and when I finish I will ask one of you to read it back to me."

With those words I transmitted the message.

A Marine Remembers

Then I called for a volunteer to read it. Private Pauling raised his hand.

"Go ahead," I told him.

Pauling read, "This class is now dismissed and will assemble here tomorrow morning at nine." They hung up their headsets and left the room.

I had given them an order and they had acted on it.

When they left the classroom I remained at my desk. I was happy about what I had accomplished, but I was also despondent. I was having second thoughts about the agreement I had made to accept the lower rating. I could just as well have been staff sergeant.

It wasn't so much the difference in pay of eight dollars a month. With my base pay of $54 a month, plus the ten percent longevity pay I was entitled to because of my prior service in the Marine Corps, my pay almost equaled that of my friend, with whom I had made the agreement. It was the housing allowance that made the difference. As staff sergeant, I would have been entitled to housing for my wife and child. As a plain sergeant, I was not.

In the regular Marine Corps, no enlisted man below the rank of staff sergeant or platoon sergeant, as the case may be, was permitted to marry without the written permission of the Marine Corps. If a Marine with a lower rating did marry without that express permission he was kicked out of the Corps. He was issued either an Undesirable Discharge or a Discharge

Samuel Rimler

For The Convenience Of The Government.

The Marine Corps Reserves were different. In the reserves even privates could marry, or could be married upon enlistment. But until or unless they achieved a higher rating than that of sergeant, they were not entitled to a housing allowance.

Of course, I reminded myself, when I made that arrangement with my friend, the battalion was still based at the Brooklyn Navy Yard and I still lived at home. Housing allowance then was not an issue. But now, living away from home, it was. I was no longer earning—scratching out—a living on the outside. So I sat at my desk and brooded.

It was nearing 1700 and almost time for evening chow. What's been done can't be undone, I told myself. I took a deep breath and sighed. Then, rising from my chair, I left for the mess hall.

The Sin of Omission

It was the spring of 1941 and my battalion was at Guantanamo Bay, Cuba undergoing rigorous training. By day the hot tropical sun beat down on us as flies attached themselves to our wet uniforms. At night the mosquitoes took over. It was not the kind of duty the men had foreseen when they had joined the reserve battalion.

"When's it all gonna end?" a young Ma-

A Marine Remembers

rine asked me one day during a break in the regimen.

"I wish I could tell you," I replied. I had been wondering the same thing. When was it gonna end? I had lost twenty pounds since our arrival and was down to a hundred and forty pounds. It wasn't as if there wasn't enough food to eat, it was that it was so bad I couldn't eat it.

I felt sorry for them. I was ten years older than many of them, knew them by their first names and, because of my previous service in the Marine Corps, they looked up to and relied on me.

"Did you hear the latest scuttlebutt, Sarge?" another young Marine asked.

"No," I said.

"We're going to have pork chops for noon chow—no kidding, they're wheeling out a field kitchen and are going to serve pork chops, green peas and mashed potatoes."

"Tell you what," I laughed, "if we have pork chops for noon chow, you can have mine."

"No kidding?" the young Marine asked unbelievingly.

"No kidding," I promised.

"What'll I give you in return?"

"You can give me your mashed potatoes," I said and forgot about the matter.

As it turned out, scuttlebutt had it right. Shortly before noon, a field kitchen came rolling out into the boondocks and the smell of pork chops permeated the air. Suddenly, I remembered my promise. But when I got into the chow line, the pork chops smelled so good. And the closer I got to the field kitchen the better they smelled.

The young Marine was some thirty feet behind me. I looked back at him to determine if he remembered my promise. It seemed that he did because he was looking in my direction.

Suddenly, I decided not to relinquish my pork chop. I even began to resent the young Marine who expected me to do so.

I decided that once I got my pork chop ration I would hurry away and eat it before he, who was fifteen men behind me in the chow line, could catch up with me. That way I could say I had forgotten my promise.

But I had underestimated the speed at which the men were being hustled through the line. By the time I had reached a spot away from the field kitchen and had settled down to savor the pork chop, there he was, standing over me with his mashed potatoes.

I took umbrage. Why did he have to track me down? Why couldn't he have taken the hint? Why was it necessary for him to have two pork chops and deprive me of one?

"Sarge," the young Marine began but I cut him short. "I've changed my mind," I said.

He walked off in silence. After that, the pork chop didn't taste as good as it had smelled.

A Marine Remembers

The Reluctant Chief

After being discharged from the Marine Corps Reserves in the summer of 1941, I applied for, and was accepted by, Civil Service to work for the Navy in the communication department in what was then being organized as Headquarters, Eastern Sea Frontier, located at 90 Church Street, New York. Because of my prior service and experience as a radioman in the Marine Corps, I was appointed supervisor of the teletypewriter room.

At the time of my appointment, my job wasn't much to speak of. I oversaw a group of civilian employees who had formerly worked for Western Union and Postal Telegraph, one or two of them still so employed, but moonlighting. Each felt that he should have been the supervisor. They attended the typewriters, sent and received messages, and griped. I had all I could do to keep them from punching each other's time cards. They resented the work and their resentment showed.

After Pearl Harbor, a group of WAVES was assigned to complement the civilian group. The communication room also received a few chiefs who had come out of retirement and were dubbed "retreads." A Navy lieutenant was put in charge. (There were no radio communications because all communications originated from, and were addressed to, land stations.) As soon as the officer arrived he quickly sized up the situation and there was no longer any griping by the civilians.

The lieutenant, well aware of my two prior enlistments in the Marine Corps and my knowledge of radio communications, urged me to enlist in the Navy, promising me a chief's rating. I hedged. My first loyalty had always been to the Marine Corps. After Pearl Harbor, I had visited a Marine Corps recruiting station and inquired as to what kind of rating I could expect if I re-enlisted. The best that was offered me was sergeant—the same rating I had held when I left. So I had declined. And now I was being offered a chief's rating, three pay grades above that of sergeant. The lieutenant kept after me, pointing out that I could still do the same job at the same place without fear of being transferred to God knows where. Finally, I admitted to him that I didn't think I was capable of holding down a chief's job because I knew nothing about maintenance. I confessed that although I was up on radio communication and Navy procedure, I didn't know the difference between a radio tube and a light bulb.

"That's no problem," the lieutenant assured me. They now had a new rating in the Navy, that of radio technician and I would have no need to know anything at all about the technical part of the work.

After a number of discussions, I finally agreed to enlist in the Navy, but only as a 1st class radioman (I would try to make chief on my own, I said), with the provision that I be transferred to sea duty. I didn't feel like sitting out the war at 90 Church Street.

The lieutenant, who would soon be on his way to Europe to join Eisenhower's staff, reluctantly agreed, although he told me I was making a mistake not accepting the chief's rating.

A Marine Remembers

The Retreads and the WAVES

Shortly after being sworn into the Navy as a radioman 1st class and still in charge of the communication center at Headquarters Eastern Sea Frontier (the communication officer had urged me to accept the rating of chief radioman but I refused, believing I wasn't qualified), the retreads and WAVES began to arrive.

The retreads were chiefs who had retired from the Navy years before but were called back to duty after Pearl Harbor. Too old to go to sea, places were found for them at shore stations where they could make themselves useful as needs arose. The WAVES were a group of young women who had volunteered for Navy service. Headquarters Eastern Sea Frontier, located at 90 Church Street, New York, with Vice Admiral Adolphus Andrews in overall command, was a teletype communication center between shore stations along the East Coast. No radio communications were used or necessary.

Four retreads and six WAVES were assigned to the communication center. One of the retreads let it be known that henceforth, because of his seniority, he would be in charge of the communication facility while the others were to blend in with the rest of the personnel, helping wherever there was a need and keeping a low profile.

Of the six WAVES who arrived, one, an attractive Italian girl in her early twenties and a second class petty officer, caught my eye. And, I believed, she was attracted to me as well.

But although we spent as much time together at the communication center as was feasible under the circumstances, no words of endearment, no touching, no mentioning of the way we felt was ever hinted at or apparent to any outside observer. We were just good friends. One day, and without prior warning, Admiral Adolphus Andrews, accompanied by his aide, Richard Barthelmess (an old time silent movie star, now a lieutenant in the Navy) and Bernard Baruch (a tall and distinguished looking man wearing a hearing aid) came to inspect the premises. After I showed them around, Bernard Baruch, who had recently donated a million dollars for Army and Navy relief, turned to me and inquired, "What is your function at this facility?"

Although nominally still in charge, I caught the eye of the retread who had assumed command and replied, "Sir, my function here is to assist the chief in charge at this communication center." That reply not only satisfied the distinguished visitors but seemed to satisfy the retread as well.

After I was transferred to sea, my friendship with the Italian WAVE continued by way of correspondence and in none of the letters were our personal feelings toward each other ever mentioned. We just remained good friends.

Her last letter was dated shortly before VJ Day and our correspondence ended when the war ended.

A Marine Remembers

The Blackboard

When I boarded the USS *Cincinnati* at the Brooklyn Navy Yard, I discovered to my chagrin that the senior radioman aboard was a 2nd class radioman and that I would have to take charge of the radio room, including all the men assigned to it and the radar-men as well. I cursed my bad luck.

I had expected to find a chief radioman aboard who would tell me what to do. And now I was the one who would have to tell others what to do. In effect, I was assigned a chief's job without the rank or privileges. I had been offered the rating and had turned it down.

It was expected that I take charge. After all, I was a 1st class radioman, I wore the two hash marks to which I was entitled because of my Marine Corps service, and my service record book noted that I had, under a vice-admiral, been in charge of communications at Headquarters, Eastern Sea Frontier.

What my service record book failed to note was that all I had been in charge of was the teletypewriter room staffed by a handful of civilians and several WAVES who were supplementing the civilian personnel.

Fortunately for me, I had stood radio watches aboard the battleships *Wyoming* and *Arkansas* and had learned how radio rooms aboard Navy vessels functioned. So I pretty well knew what had to be done. Thus, when the communication officer asked me if I had any problems, I said none that I couldn't handle. Then I asked the communication officer if there were any problems I should be made aware of. By then, a radio officer and a chief warrant officer had been assigned to join us.

There was the problem of the blackboard, the communication officer said. "A blackboard?" I asked unbelievingly. Yes, a blackboard was the reply. It seemed that they had tried every which way to get a blackboard to use in instructing the strikers (beginners), but without success.

"If I have your permission to leave the ship, I'll see what I can do about it," I said.

The three officers looked at me dubiously. The communication officer said, "You have my permission."

I walked down the gangplank and found my way to the carpenter shop. There, I sought out the foreman and introduced myself. "My ship is getting underway at 1800 today and we need a blackboard. I gave him the dimensions. "When can we have it?" It was then 1100.

"You will have it by 1300," the shop foreman promised.

"Can I count on it?" I inquired.

"You have my word for it," was the reply.

At 1250, while the three officers and I were leaning over the rail of the ship, the officers eyeing me doubtfully, and my heart thumping, two civilians made their appearance carrying the blackboard. My first day aboard ship and my reputation had been made.

A Marine Remembers

The Message

    I had never questioned an order before. Whether the order was to clean garbage cans on Parris Island with the flies buzzing around me, or to spot shellfire on the coast of North Africa with shells whirling about me, I had never questioned it. But this time I tried—and failed.
    I was lying on my bunk in the chief's quarters, fully dressed during a crossing of the North Atlantic, trying to steal an hour's sleep. The weather was especially bad and the seas were rough, so I lay on my bunk spread-eagled to keep from being tossed out of it. I had just about dozed off when I felt someone shake me. I opened my eyes.
    "What's up?" I asked the yeoman standing over me.
    "The communication officer wants to see you," was the reply.
    "Now?" I asked resentfully.
    "Right now, Chief."
    I groaned and got out of my bunk. Making my way to the radio room, I looked questioningly at the supervisor of the watch who shrugged his shoulders. When I walked into the adjoining code room, I found the communication officer, the radio officer and a chief warrant officer waiting for me with somber expressions on their faces. What have I done now? I asked myself. What have I failed to do?
    "Chief, I have a message for you to send," the communication officer said.
    I was relieved and alarmed at the same time. Relieved to know I had done nothing wrong and

alarmed at the thought of breaking radio silence.

"Are we breaking radio silence?" I asked in disbelief.

"We're breaking radio silence," was the reply.

My mind began to race. Alarm bells were going off. It wasn't as if this would be a plain-language message where if a letter was missed it could be filled in to complete a word. This was a coded message where one missed letter or numeral could garble the text, making the message impossible to decode.

The weather was bad. Transmission facilities were bad. There was much static. IMIs (repeats) might be requested, furthering transmission time and, thus, the chance that U-boats would pick up the radio signals. I was hesitant to accept the responsibility.

"I'll give it to the 1st-class to send," I said.

"If I wanted the 1st-class to send it I wouldn't have sent for you," the communication officer said.

"He's all right," I assured the communication officer. "He's got a good fist—there's nothing to worry about."

"I don't think I've made myself clear," the communication officer said. "I want you to send it."

I was worried when I took the message from the communication officer. He looked the way I felt. He and the other officers were even more somber than before. They were aware of the risks just as I was. The difference was that the responsibility was mine.

My heart was pounding and my lips were

A Marine Remembers

white when I walked into the radio room. For the first time, I looked at the message and examined the heading. It was addressed to Washington. That was good, I thought. Only the best radio operators were stationed there. It was marked "urgent." That was to be expected; otherwise they wouldn't be breaking radio silence to send it. The text consisted of forty coded words grouped in five jumbled letters to the word.

I displaced one of the radiomen on watch, sat down in my place and tuned the transmitter to the proper frequency. The three officers had followed me into the radio room and were now standing behind me watching, anxiety written on their faces.

It's just another message, I told myself. You've sent dozens of them under ordinary circumstances. Make believe these are ordinary circumstances. Make believe you're teaching at Quantico. Make believe you're just practicing. But these weren't ordinary circumstances and I couldn't make believe. The imperative was to send the message in the shortest possible time. That didn't mean at the fastest rate of speed I was capable of. It did mean the fastest way without risking requests for repeats. I decided on 18 to 20 words a minute.

There was stillness in the radio room that nobody dared break as I placed my hand on the transmission key. Offering a short silent prayer, I sent: NAA V NITR AR (Chief of Naval Operations from USS *Cincinnati* waiting to hear from you) and held my breath.

In fewer than five seconds the answer was NITR V NAA K (USS *Cincinnati* from Chief of Naval

Operations go ahead).

So far, so good, I thought. I sent the heading, paused a second, and continued with the text at my chosen rate of speed. I held my breath. Please God, I thought, no IMIs.

In less than five seconds I copied: NITR V NAA R (USS *Cincinnati* from Chief of Naval Operations, received).

The sigh of relief emitted by all present in the radio room broke the room's stillness.

I looked at my watch. The transmission had taken less than three minutes. But it was the longest three minutes I had ever experienced.

The Circumcision

The two medical officers aboard ship were far removed in rank, but it was the junior medical officer who, to all intents and purposes, was the doctor, patients seeking him out to the exclusion of the senior medical officer.

Why a lieutenant commander in the Navy should be looked down on by both officers and enlisted men, I was never able to determine. Perhaps it had to do with his previous occupation. It was rumored that before the war he had worked for the Red Cross as a first aid man while the lieutenant (jg), two ranks his junior, had enjoyed a successful private practice on the outside. In any event, it was none of my business and I made no attempt to find out.

But I felt sorry for the man. First, for be-

A Marine Remembers

ing ignored and sometimes poked fun at behind his back, and second, because his rank was not being respected. I had always respected rank.

Consequently, whenever we happened to come into contact, I greeted him courteously and paid him his due respect. And he appreciated it. It gave him a lift to have a chief petty officer pay him homage when all others aboard ship held him in disdain. As he once complained to me, "Here am I, a lieutenant commander in the Navy, and nobody gives a goddamn."

During a crossing of the North Atlantic, my duties were so many and varied and took up so much of my time, that I found little time for rest. Nor did putting out the ship's daily morning news sheets help my situation. The news items sent by Reuters, United Press, and Associated Press were transmitted at thirty-five words a minute and I was the only radioman aboard ship who could copy that fast. To further complicate matters, the yeoman to whom I turned over the copy made errors in editing and in cutting the stencils. So I, being particular about my work, had to do those jobs myself. Because all this work had to be done in the small hours of the morning, I had little time for sleep. Finally, I reached a point where I could no longer function—I was completely exhausted.

"Why don't you check into the sick bay for a couple of days?" the communication officer suggested when I advised him of my situation.

"What about the captain?" I asked. "He'll miss the news reports."

"I'll see to the captain," the communication officer promised.

I checked into the sick bay that night and for the first time in longer than I could remember I had a good night's sleep. During morning sick call, the junior medical officer came to my cot, examined me, and remarked, "In another day or two you'll be as good as new." Then he held sick call for the other sailors who had filtered into the room. When he finished with them, a last sailor walked into the sick bay, a boatswain's mate who wanted to be circumcised. The doctor told the pharmacist's mate to get him ready for the operation while he went into the wardroom and had a cup of coffee.

The pharmacist's mate bade the sailor to lie down on an operating table, had him pull his pants and skivvy shorts down below his knees, and doused his parts with iodine, telling him to stay put until the doctor returned.

Just then, the senior medical officer entered the sick bay and, seeing the sailor stretched out on the table, inquired of the pharmacist's mate about the situation, the sailor eyeing him warily all the time.

When the senior medical officer was informed, he rubbed his hands together and exclaimed, "Gee, a circumcision. I haven't done one of these in a long time. I think I'll do this one."

"The hell you will," the boatswain's mate said, pulling his pants up and skedaddling out of the sick bay.

My rest was short-lived. The captain had been irate for not having received his morning news sheets and had warned the communication officer never to let that happen again. That same night, I was back in the radio room compiling my ten-page news reports.

The Fire at Sea

It was winter and the waters of the North Atlantic were at their worst when my ship, the USS *Cincinnati*, heading a convoy of cargo vessels and tankers, caught fire. The convoy and its six destroyer escorts (DEs) were ordered to proceed, leaving the lead ship behind to extinguish the flames.

The convoy could proceed no faster than its slowest ship. This was a tanker with its midships half underwater, traveling at eight to ten knots per hour. Our ship was a light cruiser and could do twenty-two knots under extreme duress, so it was hoped that we would catch up with the rest of the convoy as soon as the flames were under control.

Meanwhile, with the convoy out of sight, the *Cincinnati* lay to like a lame duck, wallowing in the turbid waters, an easy prey for any German U-boat that happened to be in the vicinity, while the seamen fighting the fires in the engine room did their best to contain the fire and keep it from spreading.

The reason for ordering the convoy ahead was obvious. It was better to have one ship at risk than to have other ships in the convoy laying to, placing them at risk as well. Nor could any of the DEs be spared to stand by our stricken ship. They were the sheep dogs guarding their flock over a wide area and they had all they could do to keep them from straying.

All divisions aboard the stricken *Cincinnati* were at their abandon ship stations, clad in life jackets, many of the men not bothering to tie the straps of their jackets. The ship carried no life boats and the chance of being rescued, should it founder, was non-existent. So, many of the men decided it would be better at such a time to divest themselves of their life jackets and die a quick death in the icy waters than linger on to suffer a worse death.

The men of "C" Division, of which I was the nominal senior petty officer ("C" Division consisted of the ship's signalmen, radiomen, radar men and yeomen, but I had no direct control over the signalmen and yeomen), like the other ship's divisions, were at their abandon ship stations. But unlike the officers of the division and me who had the straps of our life jackets tied to set an example for the men, many of the men of the division abstained from doing so. Rather then admonishing them for this dereliction, I, as well as the officers, chose to look away.

And so they remained at their abandon ship stations, helplessly awaiting their fate as the ship wallowed in the sea. After a time, however, the firemen down below proved equal to their task and the fire was contained and then extinguished. The men returned to their duties, the ship got under way and eventually we caught up with the rest of the convoy, which continued on its way.

A Marine Remembers

What impressed me during this incident was that, although there was much concern depicted in the faces of the men, there was no panic, no outward show of fear.

The Moral Binding

I stood gazing out the window of my third floor Division Avenue apartment. It was bitter cold and from where I stood I could see the ship's superstructure. She was tied up at the Brooklyn Navy Yard and every foot of her was covered with ice. I watched the icicles on her masts glistening in the reflected moonlight.

She was an old and tired ship and top-heavy as well. When she was commissioned in 1922, radar and direction finder antennas were unknown, additional gun emplacements were not needed, and the spotting plane she carried was still a figment of the imagination.

Convoying in the North Atlantic was the worst kind of duty and no medals were awarded for it. On our last crossing, the ship had lost its spotting plane, all its life rafts, and two men. One man was washed overboard and the other had his head crushed after he was hurled from one end of the engine room to the other. The ship might have suffered a third casualty in the radio room had I not broken the momentum of one of the radiomen who had been thrown across the room. As it was, he suffered a broken ankle when he was struck by the typewriter that followed him.

And I could have avoided it all. As a civilian supervisor of communications at Headquarters, Eastern Sea Frontier, I was free from the draft and safely ensconced in a warm building on Church Street. Even after enlisting in the Navy, I could have had the same job for the duration, eating at the Automat, and sleeping at home. Yet I had enlisted and then requested sea duty. Why?

It was a question I asked myself many times. I asked it every time the ship listed forty-five degrees in heavy weather. I asked it when sea water swished two decks below the water line, shorting out the ovens so the cooks couldn't cook and the bakers couldn't bake. I asked it during U-boat activity when it was anybody's guess which ship of the convoy would disappear under the waves.

And yet I had enlisted and requested sea duty. If I hadn't done so, what difference would it have made? Who would have known? Who would have cared? The answer was always the same. I would have known. I would have cared. It would have made a difference to me.

Six months before Pearl Harbor, I had left the Marine Corps Reserve while on active duty. I knew that I should have remained. I was an ex-Marine, a communicator. I was needed. But I left.

How could I have remained? My wife

A Marine Remembers

had given birth to a baby daughter the week I received my orders. How could I hope to support a wife and baby on a sergeant's pay of fifty-four dollars a month? And so I left and had ever since thought of myself as a summer patriot—a fair weather soldier. And it wasn't a pleasant thought.

After Pearl Harbor, the communications officer at the Eastern Sea Frontier offered me a chance to redeem myself. He induced me to come into the Navy, offering me a chief petty officer's rating, and assuring me that I would remain at the same job, performing the same duties. I refused the chief petty officer's rating thinking I wasn't qualified, accepted a rating one step down, and requested sea duty.

My wife was asleep in bed and the baby asleep in her crib as I continued to gaze out the window. My ship was due to get underway at 0800 and it was now 0100 and I felt sorry for myself. I was, again, about to exchange the warmth and safety of a loving home for the danger and cruelty of the sea. But what else was there to do?

I walked away from the window, took a last look at my wife asleep in bed and the baby in the crib, turned up the collar of my pea coat, and quietly left the house.

Samuel Rimler

The Chiefs

After convoying the North Atlantic and after covering the invasion of southern France, my ship was ordered to patrol the South Atlantic in conjunction with the Brazilian Navy.

This change of duty was a relief from the harrowing experiences of the past two years. With liberty in ports like Recife, Bahia and Rio, it was the kind of duty that sailors ship over for. After this brief respite, however, my ship received orders to transfer one chief radioman to Boston to board the new USS *Helena* (the old one had been sunk by the Japanese) for duty in the South Pacific. Since I was the only chief radioman aboard, the order was directed at me.

The communication officer suggested that they promote the first class radioman to chief and send him, but I pointed out that the first class lacked the experience to board a new ship and take charge of a new radio room with a new crew. So I volunteered to go and let the first class remain aboard, where he would be subsequently promoted to chief.

When I arrived in Boston, the USS *Helena* was not yet ready for its shakedown cruise, so I applied for and received twenty days' leave. Upon my return from leave, my orders had been changed. My new orders read that I was to go to Guantanamo Bay, Cuba and take charge of the radio station at the Navy base there.

When I arrived at Guantanamo, I reported to the communication officer, a reserve lieutenant who was new to the Navy.

A Marine Remembers

"I hope you can straighten this mess out," he told me.

"What mess?" I asked.

"You'll find out," the communication officer said.

I did find out—and in a hurry. When I walked into the radio room, I couldn't believe what I saw. The place was a mess. The men were unkempt and lax in the performance of their duties. Most of them, the highest rating a second class radioman, had been stationed at the base during their entire Navy service and considered the place their home away from home. With no one to supervise them, they thought that that's the way things were done.

I put them straight in a hurry. I assembled the motley gang and laid down the law. I told them I was going to post certain rules and regulations on a bulkhead inside the radio room. I told them that there were ships in the harbor leaving for the South Pacific every day. I told them that anyone who disobeyed a posted order would find himself on one of those ships within twenty-four hours. Within forty-eight hours of my arrival, the matter of the radio room had been set straight. The communication officer couldn't believe the metamorphosis.

"I have one more problem, Chief," the communication officer confided.

"Anything I can do to help?" I inquired.

"I don't know," the communication officer said doubtfully.

"Try me."

"As you no doubt know by now, we have four frequencies to guard, but only three radio receivers."

"I noticed that. Have you made out a requisition for another one?"

"I have, time and again, but they seem to get lost."

"I'll see what I can do," I promised.

I found my way to the supply depot. It was a block-long building with a vast store of equipment and supplies. I introduced myself to the chief storekeeper and we exchanged a few pleasantries.

"What can I do for you?" he asked.

"I need a radio receiver," I said.

"Have you got a requisition?"

"No."

"Then I can't let you have one."

"Chief," I said, "do you know how many radio receivers you have in this warehouse?"

"No," he admitted.

""Does the chief supply officer know?"

"I don't believe so."

"Does the base commander know?"

"Not that I'm aware of."

"Does anybody know?"

"I see your point," the chief storekeeper said. "You can have your radio receiver. By the way," he said in parting, "what would the Navy do without us chiefs?"

"I guess they'd have to invent us," I replied.

A Marine Remembers

Brother, Can You spare a Cigarette?

I had never had any desire to smoke. When I was a teenager on the Lower East Side a friend urged me to try it, but after taking a couple of puffs on a Lucky Strike and almost choking to death, I never tried again.

In the Navy I could buy a pack for five cents or a carton for half a dollar. I would buy them and send them home to my father and my wife, both of whom were smokers. I myself had never wanted a cigarette—except this time.

I was walking along the streets of Miami after leaving the USS *Cincinnati*. I was waiting for transportation to Boston to board the new USS *Helena* (the old one had been sunk by the Japs). I had been flown to Miami in a NATS transport from Bahia, and after stops at Rio de Janeiro and Trinidad, was awaiting transportation to my new assignment. So I had time to waste and I wasted it by walking along the streets of Miami.

Earlier, I had gone to the movies to see Jack Benny in *The Horn Blows at Midnight*. I hadn't much cared for it. Whoever sold Jack Benny on that film had made a bad sale. But admission for a serviceman in uniform was free so it wasn't much of a loss to me. The loss was to Jack Benny's reputation.

As I walked down one of the main steets, I noticed someone following me. I paused and looked back. He was a well-dressed middle-aged man, about a hundred feet behind me. When I stopped, he stopped.

Samuel Rimler

When I continued walking, he continued walking. Finally, after two more such incidents, my curiosity got the best of me. I walked back to where he was standing and asked, "Why are you following me?"

"Please, Chief," the man asked, "can you spare a cigarette?"

I looked at him, embarrassed. The one time I wanted a cigarette, I didn't have one. I would gladly have given the man a pack—or a carton, for that matter—because I knew how difficult cigarettes were to buy. But I had none to give.

"I'm sorry, sir, but I don't smoke," I said. Then I said, "Wait" and the man's eyes lit up.

I looked about me trying to find a serviceman, any uniform, trying to get the man a cigarette. But hard as I looked I could see no other serviceman around. I again apologized. The poignant look in the man's eyes was painful to see.

The Kiss

I had volunteered to leave a comparatively safe haven patrolling the South Atlantic aboard the USS *Cincinnati* for the USS *Helena*, still to be commissioned at the Boston Navy Yard, thereafter to be ordered for duty in the South Pacific where the war with Japan was still raging.

I didn't have to volunteer for that assignment, just as I needn't have volunteered to enlist in the Navy or, having enlisted, gone to sea. But these things I'd done willingly.

A Marine Remembers

During the war I had done duty in the North and South Atlantic and in the Mediterranean and Caribbean, but never in the Pacific.

The farthest west I had been in the Pacific was in peacetime while still in the Marine Corps, when my ship, the USS *Arkansas*, had taken a contingent of Annapolis midshipmen to the Hawaiian Islands for a training cruise.

I looked forward to the task of taking charge of the radio room on the new heavy cruiser. The *Cincinnati* had been a top-heavy light cruiser commissioned in 1922. The *Helena* would be a change for the better.

That the war was still raging in the Pacific never entered my mind. It wasn't as though I wasn't concerned. But long ago I had made up my mind not to be scared until there was something to be scared of and I tried to live by that doctrine.

When I arrived at the Boston Navy Yard, the *Helena* had not yet been commissioned, so I applied for and received twenty days' leave, something I had not received since joining the Navy, and to which I was entitled.

Upon my return from leave, I found that my orders had been changed. I was now to proceed by the first available transportation to the Navy base at Guantanamo Bay, where I would take charge of the radio station.

As I stood on the Boston train platform awaiting the train that would take me to New York, I noticed two girls in their late teens some thirty feet from me, whispering to one another. I turned my head away in amusement. They were probably talking about their boyfriends

When I next turned my head their way one of them came over, stood directly in front of me, and kissed me full on the lips. Then, without saying a word, she ran back to her companion and they both disappeared from sight.

For the longest time following the incident, I wondered whether their whispered discussion pertained to which of them should kiss me or which should avoid doing so.

The Passenger

I had been in charge of the radio station at the Guantanamo naval base for a number of weeks and in that time had put things right—so much so that the base commander had commended the communication officer for the efficient way the department was run and I had been appointed to the commodore's staff. I was to board all new constructions that came to the base for their shakedown cruises.

My job was to go to a ship's radio room and see that periodicals were up to date and that proper procedures were being followed. In a way, the situation was a bit of an embarrassment to me. Being on the commodore's staff, I had the power to approve or disapprove the manner in which a ship's radio room functioned. Officers far above my rank treated me with respect not ordinarily due me. They knew that my report would be a reflection on them and their department, that it would reach the eyes

A Marine Remembers

of the commodore, and that it could require further training and, thus, delay their ship's departure.

That was the situation when one morning my communication officer called me into his office, a dour expression on his face.

"Anything wrong, sir?" I inquired.

The communication officer handed me a service record book. "What do you think?" he asked.

I examined it closely. It was the service record book of a chief radioman who had made chief a month before I had. "I see, sir" I said.

"He should be arriving any day now. What can we do about it?"

The implication of the new arrival was clear. In the Navy, as in all other branches of the service, seniority was everything. The new arrival would have to take over. I didn't like the idea and it was plain to see that the communication officer didn't like it either. Things were running too smoothly.

"Unless the man happens to be incompetent or unreliable, I guess I'll have to step aside," I said.

"Do you think that's likely?"

"Hardly. No incompetent person would achieve that rank."

The communication officer took a deep breath. "We'll have to play it by ear," he said. But it was plain to see he was worried.

And I was worried too. I didn't feel like stepping aside for anyone. I had worked too hard to achieve my present status. I decided that when the other arrived, I would request a transfer to one of the ships in the harbor headed for the South Pacific.

But we needn't have worried. When the new chief arrived a few days later, he no more wanted to take charge of anything than he wanted to fly to the moon.

He, a tall Texan, walked into the radio room and introduced himself. I took him outside and said, "I'll brief you about what's going on."

"I don't want to know what's going on," was his surprising rejoinder.

"But you have to know. You're here."

"Make believe I'm not here."

As it turned out, the communication officer didn't want to know he was there either and they avoided each other at every opportunity.

But the new chief turned out to be a barrel of laughs. He had a droll sense of humor and the circumstances under which he had been dumped at Guantanamo were unbelievably comical.

As he related the story, he had never been to sea but had spent the war years working contentedly at a teletype communication center on the east coast. One day, a destroyer escort pulled into port minus a chef radioman and since he was the only chief radioman on the premises, he was shanghaied to fill the slot. He boarded the DE in the evening and the ship was soon underway to pick up a convoy for the North Atlantic. He no sooner located his bunk when he became seasick and crawled into it, remaining there during the entire crossing and return, leaving it only to go to the head. Upon

A Marine Remembers

the ship's return to home port, the communication officer sought him out, told him, "Chief, we do not carry passengers," and kicked him off the ship. During his entire stay aboard ship, he never even entered the radio room or became aware of its location.

The Captain and the Chiefs

It had happened the day of my arrival at Guantanamo. I didn't know what had happened, how it happened, why it happened, or who made it happen. But it had happened.

Scuttlebutt had it that one of the chiefs stationed on the base had come back from liberty at Guantánamo City inebriated, had gone into the chiefs' head (washroom), and had put his fist through a mirror above a wash basin, breaking it. And I, a new arrival on the base was being punished for it. Not that it really mattered. I had no intention of going to Guantánamo City. One went there for women and whiskey and I didn't drink and didn't want anything to do with the prostitutes.

During his inspection, the captain, spotting the broken mirror, demanded to know the name of the culprit. Those chiefs who didn't know, couldn't tell and those who knew, wouldn't. To find out, all the captain needed to do was examine the fists of all the chiefs stationed on the base. But he either didn't think of this or had no intention of looking at the fists of some sixty chiefs: 120 fists in all. So he issued the following instructions:

Samuel Rimler

1. Effective immediately, all Chief Petty Officers are denied the privileges of the CPO Recreation Center and all other facilities selling or dispensing intoxicating beverages on the Naval Station, Naval Air Station, or Marine Site, and are to be in their quarters at taps.
2. The Barracks Officer will muster these Chief Petty Officers at taps each night and see that they are all present or accounted for. There will be no absentees except those Chiefs on a duty status. Any absentees will be reported by the Barracks Officer to the Executive Officer, Naval Station.
3. This restriction will remain in effect until the incident of destruction of Government property in the CPO Head has been cleaned up.
4. Bay Hill Duty Officer will also give barracks close supervision to prevent any infraction of the above restriction.

G. E. Sage
Captain, U.S. Navy
Commanding

Distribution:

All Chief Petty Officers
First Lieutenant; Barracks Office
Bay Hill Duty Officers
Training Group: SubDiv 72

Note: The above memorandum was in effect until after V.J. Day but no one paid any attention to it.

A Marine Remembers

The Enigma

  I sat on my bunk in the chief petty officers' quarters. I was in a quandary. It was ten days after V.J. Day and everyone with enough points was scrambling to get out of the service. If the trend continued, the Navy would find itself with ships but no men to service them. I had enough points to get out. But should I?
  At the Guantanamo Bay Naval Base where I was stationed, I was well thought of and highly regarded, so much so that I had become a unit of the commodore's staff. I wanted for nothing. I had been urged by my superiors to remain in the Navy. But should I? With my eleven years of broken service, it would mean that I would have to spend nineteen more years in the Navy to be eligible for retirement. Did I want that? Especially since I had gone as far as I could go in the enlisted ranks and wasn't eligible for a commission.
  It was the third time in my military career that I was pondering such a decision. And it was no easier this time than before.
  The first time had been in 1934 over the ham sandwich incident. More than once I wished I had eaten that sandwich. If I'd eaten it there wouldn't have been a grease stain on the back of my pack, my captain wouldn't have called me on it, I wouldn't have revenged myself on him by insisting on a transfer, and I would have remained in the Marine Corps. But would I be alive today? It was doubtful. More than half my unit had died on Guadalcanal.

Samuel Rimler

The second time was the summer of 1941, when, after enlisting in the Marine Corps Reserves, my unit was called to active duty. By then I had a wife and baby to support on my sergeant's pay of fifty-four dollars a month. After deducting a few dollars a month for my personal needs, could my wife and baby survive on the balance of my pay? Possibly. But I didn't want to take the chance. So I had requested a discharge. Would I be alive today had I remained with my unit? Probably not.

But isn't survival a matter of chance? Since enlisting in the Navy after Pearl Harbor I had convoyed the North Atlantic at the height of the submarine activity. I had covered the invasion of southern France from a French tug, spotting shellfire a hundred yards off the French coast in rough Mediterranean waters. I was on the beach in North Africa as the fleet maneuvered a dozen miles off the coast, testing their guns. Spotting shellfire, I watched their missiles soar over my head. Any of them could have fallen short of its target, putting an end to my existence. But I was still alive. Survival, I decided, *was* a matter of chance.

None of this had anything to do with my current dilemma. Should I or shouldn't I? Funny, I thought. All three decisions about staying in the service were the result of that damned ham sandwich.

A Marine Remembers

The Decision

Should I or shouldn't I? I weighed the consequences. My base pay was a hundred thirty-eight dollars a month, plus a clothing allowance and subsistence pay for my wife and daughter. In the Navy I wanted for nothing. What were my chances on the outside?

True, I could return to my job at the Eastern Sea Frontier. Congress had enacted a law guaranteeing all servicemen their jobs once the war was over. But I knew that would be short-lived. With the war over, what need was there for an Eastern Sea Frontier whose main function had been convoying and anti-submarine activity? I knew I could get my job back, but I knew also that there was no future for me there. So now what?

Had I not been married, there'd be no question about it. I'd remain in the Navy nineteen more years or thirty more years if necessary. But I had my wife and baby to think of.

As a chief, I was entitled to family quarters if my wife joined me. I had even toyed with the idea of having her and our baby daughter join me at Guantanamo. But would my wife be happy away from her family and friends? I doubted it. Also, in the Navy, as in the Marine Corps, you don't stay put, but are periodically transferred from base to base, pillar to post, so to speak, or sent to sea. What then? Would I have her follow me around the globe? And would she be able to accommodate herself to her Christian compatriots? I doubted it. My wife had told me she liked to be surrounded by Jews.

I had always gotten along with the Christian men in the Navy as well as in the Marine Corps. And they had always accepted me. But would the same be true for my wife? I doubted it.

Coming from a traditional Jewish family and used to having only Jewish friends, she would find it hard to accommodate herself to her new surroundings and make new friends. She and I were much alike in many ways but very different in others. I felt at ease amongst Christians. She felt at odds with them and, try as I would, I couldn't make her understand that in general people take you for what you are, not who you are. It's not your religion, but your behavior, that matters.

I didn't know what awaited me on the outside, but in the end I decided to leave. I knew that the Navy could better do without me than could my wife and I had no wish to cause her any unhappiness. Whether or not I had made the right decision, time would tell.

The Last Hurrah

Upon my decision to leave the Navy, I was transferred from Guantanamo Bay, Cuba to Norfolk, Virginia by destroyer escort and thence by train to Bainbridge, Maryland to await separation from the service. When I arrived there, I found a myriad of Navy personnel, both male and female, at the separation center awaiting discharge with no apparent duties to perform.

A Marine Remembers

It was nearing the end of September, 1945, and although those gathered at the separation center hoped to get out as quickly as they possibly could, my hope was to extend my Navy service to the first of October so I would be entitled to an additional month's pay and allowances. (My hope was not to be realized; I was discharged from the Navy on September 30, 1945.)

There was nothing for me to do except shoot the breeze with other chiefs and wait in chow lines. The chow lines extended for blocks and although the chiefs could head the lines, the WAVES (an acronym for Women Accepted For Voluntary Emergency Service), by virtue of their sex, no matter what their ratings, had precedence over the chiefs. No matter that a chief had two rows of service ribbons and a couple of service stripes and the WAVE was a yeoman 3rd class who had done filing in some nondescript office. The chief had to step back and make room for her.

The sailors who stood at the ends of the chow lines griped about the special treatment accorded the WAVES. But the chiefs did not complain. While the sailors had nothing to look at but the chiefs' rear ends, the chiefs, standing directly behind the WAVES, had a more interesting view.

The men who had performed important and specialized tasks at sea now had nothing to do except wait in chow lines. As soon as they got through one chow line, another one formed. This waiting around to be processed out became frustrating and they grew restive.

To solve this problem, someone in the upper chain of command conceived a brilliant idea. Jobs would be created for them. And so it came to pass.

My tall Texan friend (he was the chief radioman who had been dumped off a destroyer because, as the ship's communication officer put it, the ship did not carry passengers) had accompanied me from Guantanamo to Bainbridge and was now given the job of directing traffic at an intersection where there was no traffic.

The job created for me—which proved to be my last in the Navy—was to stand guard over a sentry whose job it was to keep sailors from sneaking into the WAVES' head. In other words, I was to make sure that the sentry himself didn't sneak into the WAVES' head.

As bad as this job was, it wasn't as bad as the one that awaited me when I returned to civilian life.

The In-Laws

I stood overlooking the bay where a dozen or more ships lay at anchor in the harbor. A wave of nostalgia had overtaken me. I had crossed the Rubicon. There was no turning back. Soon, my status would be changed. Soon, I would be changed from a something to a nothing.

As I stood there ruminating about my future, I was joined by Chief Rollins, a machinist's mate with whom I had served on the commodore's

A Marine Remembers

staff. The function of that staff had been to board vessels arriving at Guantanamo Bay for their shakedown cruises. It was our job to determine, each in our own field of expertise, if a vessel was ready to carry out the task assigned it. Chief Rollins, too, had opted to return to civilian life.

"Any plans for the future?" he asked me.

"None," I said. "What about you?"

"I'm all set," Rollins replied. "My father-in-law has offered to take me into his auto supply business."

"I wish we could exchange fathers-in-law," I said.

"That bad?"

"Judge for yourself. After my discharge from the regular Marine Corps, I somehow drifted into the wholesale egg business where I scratched out a living. From 1935 when I met his daughter to 1940 when I was activated while serving in the Marine Corps Reserves, although my father-in-law owned a number of grocery stores as well as a hotel resort in the Catskills where eggs were consumed on the premises faster than the chickens could lay them, he never offered to buy a dozen eggs from me."

"Whew," Rollins whistled. "What about the rest of the family?"

"I'll be short and to the point," I replied. "My wife has a stepmother who behaves like a stepmother. She has an older brother who had the soft drink concession in his father's hotel, where my wife slaved as a waitress, and when my three-year-old daughter begged him for a bottle of Coca Cola he chased her away, making her cry. Should I go on?"

"No, I've heard enough. You know what I would do if I were you?"

"What would you do?"

"When I got back home, I'd grab my wife and kid and run as fast and far away as I could. You live in New York? Go to California. That's three thousand miles away. Unless you want to settle in Hawaii, you can't get any farther away from them."

Grab your wife and kid and run away to California. The thought got into my head. Somehow, I would find a way.

The Friends

1.

We had met at Quantico where we were both in the same outfit. Although of different environments, temperaments, and religions, we had gravitated toward each other and had become friends.

We served aboard ship together, chased bandits in Nicaragua together, and were in turn chased by Panamanian police together. We served in Haiti together and in Puerto Rico and the Virgin Islands. Together, we patrolled the streets of Long Beach after the earthquake.

Aboard ship, we had access to each other's lockers and it was known amongst the members of the floating battalion that if an argument was picked with one of us, it was picked with both of us. At Fort

A Marine Remembers

Lewis, Washington I had borrowed his rifle when mine had malfunctioned and had qualified as an expert rifleman, a feat that netted me five dollars a month additional pay.

And then, in the fall of 1933, after serving together for two and a half years, we were about to be separated. My friend, along with a number of other men, had received orders to join the Marine forces on Wake Island.

Several days before his transfer, and while our ship was anchored off Long Beach, I had expressed an inclination to attend the High Holiday services at a synagogue in Los Angeles. Getting leave to do so, I knew, constituted no problem. I had not requested, nor had I received, any leave since joining the Marine Corps. But maintaining myself while ashore was a problem. I had no funds.

"I've got forty dollars saved you can have," my friend said.

Forty dollars. That constituted two months pay.

"I can't take your money," I responded.

"Why not?" my friend demanded to know.

"Because I don't know if, how, when, or where I can return it."

"Look," my friend said, "take the forty dollars. If you repay it, fine. If you don't, the sky won't fall."

Samuel Rimler

2.

This is the story of another friend.

We met in junior high school when I took his part when he was being picked on. Then I dropped out of school and we had lost touch. Subsequently, I enlisted in the Marine Corps and he obtained a job at a tailor supply store on Delancey Street.

When I came out of the Marine Corps, we resumed our acquaintance. By this time, he had acquired a partnership in the business with his father's financial help.

Shortly after that, my friend got married. The following year I got married, with him as best man. We two couples became quite close and spent most of our leisure time together. Neither couple made plans to go anywhere without checking with the other to see if they were free to accompany them.

Twice, I came to his aid. The first time was when his clerks picketed his store to obtain union representation. I crossed the picket line to go help out in the store.

The second was when he bought a consignment of stolen merchandise and was afraid that detectives would visit his place to investigate the robbery. He prevailed upon me to stow the stolen goods in my panel truck and keep them there until the danger was over. I obliged, knowing well that if I was caught with the goods, I risked a term in jail.

And then came Pearl Harbor. I enlisted in

A Marine Remembers

the Navy.

While risking my life convoying the North Atlantic, my friend was enriching himself doing business on the black market. While my wife was toiling as a waitress in the Catskills to supplement my meager Navy pay, my friend's wife was a regular guest at Grossinger's, enjoying her husband's ill-gotten riches. Not once during my years in the Navy did my friend or his wife check to see how my wife was faring.

Then came V.J. Day. I was discharged from the Navy with a chief petty officer's rating. I needed to go job-hunting. In order to go job-hunting I needed a decent suit of clothes. But suits were impossible to purchase. Price controls were still in effect, shortages were prevalent, and the black market was alive and well. So I walked around in my uniform, which, although respected by officers and enlisted men in the Navy, seemed to be held in disdain by people on the outside.

And then I thought of my friend who did business with tailors and clothing manufacturers. If anyone could help me buy a suit of clothes, he could. I made my way to his store, but was not made especially welcome. "What can I do for you?" he asked, after a perfunctory greeting.

"Can you use your influence to help me buy a suit of clothes?" I asked.

"Change the buttons on your uniform," my friend advised.

Samuel Rimler

The Fall From Grace

Those who haven't been in that position can never know, nor understand, the feeling of degradation of a man of rank, who, having served his country well in time of need and having been looked up to by those below him and respected by those above, must face an outside world after being separated from the service. When I left the Navy at the end of hostilities I was unappreciated, unneeded, and unwanted.

With no future to look forward to, with no outside connections, with family members either unable or unwilling to help, with former friends who had prospered on the outside turning their backs on me, without even the opportunity to purchase a suit of clothes due to the shortage of merchandise, I wondered if I had been lucky or unlucky to have survived the war.

Finally reduced to driving a taxicab, one of the least respected vocations in society, where I was harassed by the police, challenged by other cab drivers—many of whom had prison records—tongue-lashed by passengers when I inadvertently took them a block out of the way and they were obliged to pay an extra nickel in fare, I tended to despise myself as much as I believed I was despised. It did not help that I had to depend on the largesse of others to eke out a living.

The thought of judging people by the size of their tips was repugnant to me. And yet, that was exactly what I was doing. I picked and chose among them to the best of my ability.

A Marine Remembers

I remember driving past a pair of nuns who had tipped me very frugally, stopping instead for a drunken out-of-town salesman who had given me five dollars for a thirty-five cent ride. When the opportunity offered itself, I would pick up Negro passengers, knowing they would tip substantially for the privilege of being chauffeured by a white driver. I accepted no fares outside the Borough of Manhattan, knowing that passengers tipped no more for long rides than they did for short ones.

I was making money—more money than I had ever made in my life. But the job sickened me. Every time I thought of what I had been, and what I had now become I was inclined to vomit. I wanted to escape, but there was no escape. There was no way out of my dilemma.

And then, as had happened sixteen years earlier when I had stumbled across a Marine recruiting station, the Marines again came to my rescue. This time it was in the guise of a Marine buddy, then a corporal but now a chief warrant officer stationed at La Jolla, California.

When I picked him up at Pennsylvania Station (he was visiting New York) and confided in him, the chief marine gunner, after listening to my plight, told me he had a cousin in Los Angeles who had a thriving business and who would, he was sure, offer me a job and a place to stay if I would make the trip out there. On that promise, I turned in my cab and headed for Los Angeles.

Samuel Rimler

The Guilt Complex – Part I

I enlisted in the Navy after Pearl Harbor when I didn't have to.

Having been assured of a safe berth at Headquarters, Eastern Sea Frontier, located at 90 Church Street, New York, I requested sea duty when I didn't have to.

I volunteered to spot shell fire in North Africa. Any one of the shells, had it fallen short, would have made me a part of the landscape.

During the invasion of southern France, I was almost crushed to death boarding a French tug, having volunteered to spot shell fire a hundred yards off the coast.

While patrolling the South Atlantic, with liberty in such ports as Recife and Rio, I asked to transfer to the USS *Helena* for duty in the South Pacific where the war was still raging. I didn't have to do that.

Why, then, was I so conscience-stricken?

The answer was Guadalcanal.

When I enlisted in the Marine Corps Reserves, headquartered at the Brooklyn Navy Yard, I was the only one of three Marines who had seen service in the regular Marine Corps. In a way, I considered myself a big leaguer playing in the minors.

When the reserve battalion was called into active service in the early part of November, 1940, I remained with it until my Honorable Discharge in June of the following year.

Then came Pearl Harbor.

A Marine Remembers

The men of the battalion, some of whom I had helped train, were among the first American forces to launch an offensive against the up-to- then invincible Japanese at Guadalcanal and I wasn't with them. And too many of those men didn't return. And I was still here.

Some day, I told myself, I would have to re-read Stephen Crane's *The Red Badge of Courage*.

The Guilt Complex – Part II

There were movie stars who had never left the movie lots. There were public officials who had seen fit not to serve. There were nabobs who had avoided the draft. And yet, when the war was over, when the shooting had stopped, they had the temerity to sit in judgment of others, to question their loyalty. And here I was with a military and naval record the others would have given their eyeteeth to possess, cursed with a guilty conscience. Why should this be so? Would it always be so?

If only I had it to do over again. If only I hadn't requested a discharge from the Marine Corps in the summer of 1941. But how was I to know that Pearl Harbor would happen? How was anybody to know?

My battalion had been activated in the fall of 1940 and I had remained with it, accompanying it to Quantico, Puerto Rico and finally, Guantanamo Bay, Cuba. But barely six months after my discharge came Pearl Harbor. And shortly after that my reserve battalion was ordered to Guadalcanal, a place no one had ever heard of and from which few of the members of my battalion would return. And I wasn't with them. Would I ever live it down?

    Enlist in the Navy after Pearl Harbor? Forget it.

    Request sea duty convoying the North Atlantic? Forget it.

    Volunteer to spot shellfire aboard a French tug in the Mediterranean during the invasion of southern France? Forget it.

    Volunteer to go to the South Pacific when the war in Europe was nearing a conclusion? Forget it.

    I still felt like a deserter. I had deserted my battalion in time of need. And the stigma wouldn't leave me.

    If only I could be like them. If only I could be like the super-patriots--the summer soldiers who had never heard a shot fired in anger, walking straight and tall, full of patriotic fervor, self-righteously judging the patriotism of others.

    But could I be like them? I doubted it. I could no more be like them thn they could be like me.

    And so the guilt complex remained.